AF478016

# Semicollusion

# Semicollusion

**Frode Steen**

*Norwegian School of Economics
and Business Administration
5045 Bergen
Norway
frode.steen@nhh.no*

**Lars Sørgard**

*Norwegian School of Economics
and Business Administration
5045 Bergen
Norway
lars.sorgard@nhh.no*

Boston – Delft

# Foundations and Trends® in Microeconomics

*Published, sold and distributed by:*
now Publishers Inc.
PO Box 1024
Hanover, MA 02339
USA
Tel. +1-781-985-4510
www.nowpublishers.com
sales@nowpublishers.com

*Outside North America:*
now Publishers Inc.
PO Box 179
2600 AD Delft
The Netherlands
Tel. +31-6-51115274

The preferred citation for this publication is F. Steen and L. Sørgard, Semicollusion, Foundations and Trends® in Microeconomics, vol 5, no 3, pp 153–228, 2009

ISBN: 978-1-60198-334-3
© 2010 F. Steen and L. Sørgard

All rights reserved. No part of this publication may be reproduced, stored in a retrieval system, or transmitted in any form or by any means, mechanical, photocopying, recording or otherwise, without prior written permission of the publishers.

Photocopying. In the USA: This journal is registered at the Copyright Clearance Center, Inc., 222 Rosewood Drive, Danvers, MA 01923. Authorization to photocopy items for internal or personal use, or the internal or personal use of specific clients, is granted by now Publishers Inc for users registered with the Copyright Clearance Center (CCC). The 'services' for users can be found on the internet at: www.copyright.com

For those organizations that have been granted a photocopy license, a separate system of payment has been arranged. Authorization does not extend to other kinds of copying, such as that for general distribution, for advertising or promotional purposes, for creating new collective works, or for resale. In the rest of the world: Permission to photocopy must be obtained from the copyright owner. Please apply to now Publishers Inc., PO Box 1024, Hanover, MA 02339, USA; Tel. +1-781-871-0245; www.nowpublishers.com; sales@nowpublishers.com

now Publishers Inc. has an exclusive license to publish this material worldwide. Permission to use this content must be obtained from the copyright license holder. Please apply to now Publishers, PO Box 179, 2600 AD Delft, The Netherlands, www.nowpublishers.com; e-mail: sales@nowpublishers.com

## Foundations and Trends® in Microeconomics

Volume 5 Issue 3, 2009

### Editorial Board

**Editor-in-Chief:**
**W. Kip Viscusi**
*Vanderbilt University*

**Editors**

Richard Carson, UC San Diego (environmental economics)
Joseph Harrington, Johns Hopkins University (industrial organization)
Tom Kniesner, Syracuse University (labor economics)
Mark V. Pauly, University of Pennsylvania (health economics)
David Wildasin, University of Kentucky (public economics)
Peter Zweifel, University of Zurich (insurance economics)

# Editorial Scope

**Foundations and Trends® in Microeconomics** will publish survey
and tutorial articles in the following topics:

- Environmental Economics
- Contingent Valuation
- Environmental Health Risks
- Climate Change
- Endangered Species
- Market-based Policy Instruments
- Health Economics
- Moral Hazard
- Medical Care Markets
- Medical Malpractice
- Insurance economics
- Industrial Organization
- Theory of the Firm
- Regulatory Economics
- Market Structure
- Auctions
- Monopolies and Antitrust
- Transaction Cost Economics
- Labor Economics
- Labor Supply
- Labor Demand
- Labor Market Institutions
- Search Theory
- Wage Structure
- Income Distribution
- Race and Gender
- Law and Economics
- Models of Litigation
- Crime
- Torts, Contracts and Property
- Constitutional Law
- Public Economics
- Public Goods
- Environmental Taxation
- Social Insurance
- Public Finance
- International Taxation

## Information for Librarians

Foundations and Trends® in Microeconomics, 2009, Volume 5, 8 issues. ISSN
paper version 1547-9846. ISSN online version 1547-9854. Also available as a
combined paper and online subscription.

Foundations and Trends® in
Microeconomics
Vol. 5, No. 3 (2009) 153–228
© 2010 F. Steen and L. Sørgard
DOI: 10.1561/0700000034

# Semicollusion[*]

## Frode Steen[1] and Lars Sørgard[2]

[1] *Department of Economics, Norwegian School of Economics and Business Administration, Helleveien 30, 5045 Bergen, Norway, frode.steen@nhh.no*
[2] *Department of Economics, Norwegian School of Economics and Business Administration, Helleveien 30, 5045 Bergen, Norway, lars.sorgard@nhh.no*

## Abstract

The notion 'semicollusion' refers to situations where firms collude in one (or several) choice variable(s) and compete in others. For example, firms collude on prices and compete on advertising. Although the notion 'semicollusion' is not so often used explicitly, it turns out that the topic is covered extensively in the economic literature. Moreover, the phenomena 'semicollusion' seem to be present in numerous industries. The purpose of this survey is to explain how semicollusion works in theory, describe empirical studies of semicollusion, and discuss the possible welfare effects of semicollusion.

[*] We are indebted to an anonymous referee and Joseph E. Harrington, Jr. for their helpful comments on an earlier draft.

# Contents

# 1

## Introduction

Collusion and competition are well-known concepts in economic literature. A typical study would consider either the competitive outcome or the (stability of) the collusive outcome in an industry, and it might be undertaken a comparison between a competitive and a collusive outcome. But is this the only possible comparison? What about the possible combinations of competition and collusion in an industry? Could it be that firms collude, and at the same time compete? How could that work in theory? Do we observe some empirical evidence of such a mixture of competition and collusion, a market outcome we will characterize as semicollusion?

The notion "semicollusion" refers to situations where firms collude in one (or several) choice variable(s) and compete in others. For example, firms collude on prices and compete on advertising. Although the notion "semicollusion" is not so often used explicitly, it turns out that the topic is covered extensively in the economic literature. Moreover, the phenomena "semicollusion" seem to be present in numerous industries. The purpose of this survey is to explain how semicollusion works in theory, describe empirical studies of semicollusion, and discuss the possible welfare effects of semicollusion.

The monograph will start with a section where we motivate for why semicollusion is an important topic. The concept will be defined, to distinguish between collusion and semicollusion. We give some examples of what we regard as semicollusive behavior in particular industries. Moreover, we also discuss the rules of the game and which choice variables we expect firms to collude on.

In the third section we will provide a framework for understanding the mechanism at work with semicollusion. In one strand of the literature it is assumed that firms collude on prices and compete on other choice variables such as advertising, capacities, or location. However, there is also another strand of the literature where firms compete on prices and collude along other dimensions. In particular, it is assumed that firms collude on R&D. We also discuss the possible outcome with semicollusion in industries with free entry.

In Section 4 we review the empirical literature on semicollusion. There are some old, anecdotal evidence of semicollusion. For example, Scherer and Ross (1990) refer to several events in various industries. We will briefly refer to some of these cases. However, in the main part of the section we concentrate on empirical studies of the effects of semicollusion. There are empirical studies that cover various types of collusion, for example collusion on prices or collusion on R&D, and we discuss empirical studies for those outcomes that were covered in Section 3.

In Section 5 we summarize our findings. We offer some general conclusions, and discuss some issues for future research.

# 2

## What is Semicollusion?

In this section we start by giving a definition of semicollusion. This serves as a guidance for which kind of models we will discuss in the next sections. Then, we report some anecdotal evidence, suggesting that semicollusion does take place in numerous industries and therefore is an important concept. Finally, we discuss more in detail what firms collude on and what they compete on. This part serves as an important input for the distinction we will draw in the next section between colluding on prices versus colluding on non-price variables.

## 2.1 A Definition

Obviously, semicollusion is related to the concept collusion. The definition of collusion varies, but typically it is a quite broad concept. In Kaplow and Shapiro (2007) it is defined as follows:

> '*Firms seek to elevate prices and thus raise their collective profits at the expense of consumers*' (p. 1099).

In a market where firms have identical costs one way to collude can be to set price equal to monopoly price and thereby maximize joint profits. In other words, firms cooperate rather than competing. However, collusion will also cover the case where they are not able to attain the monopoly price. In fact, in a market with homogenous goods, identical costs, price setting and no capacity constraint than any price between marginal costs, and the monopoly price can be a collusive outcome. Collusion need not entail joint profit maximization. For example, joint profit maximization might not be reasonable if firms are asymmetric and transfers are not allowed. As described in Kaplow and Shapiro (2007), firms coordinate their activities on several dimensions other than fixing prices. They not only limit their production, but in many cases they allocate customers and territories among themselves.

The economic concept collusion covers all cases where prices are raised above a competitive level. The outcome is crucial for defining collusion, and not the way firms have behaved in order to succeed with collusion. This implies that collusion covers both the case where firms have colluded tacitly and the case where collusion between firms is explicit.[1] The latter is often denoted cartels, where firms, for example, have had meetings to agree on how to fix prices.

The legal approach to collusion differs from the economic approach. It is a narrower concept, where collusion covers only cases where firms have communicated in a specific way and where collusion of that type is illegal per se. This implies that direct communication, for example through meetings, is illegal while collusion with no kind of communication (tacit collusion) is legal. Unfortunately, in the gray area in between tacit collusion on the one hand and cartels supported by meetings where they fix prices on the other hand, it is still a lot of uncertainty concerning the distinction between legal and illegal collusion.[2]

---

[1] See, for example, Levenstein and Suslow (2008) for a discussion of the concept. The idea that firms could attain the monopoly outcome without explicit collusion was first discussed in Chamberlin (1929). See also Tirole (1988), Chapter 6, for a discussion of the notion tacit collusion.

[2] According to European case law illegal collusion takes place if concerted practice can be proven, i.e., it can be proven that there is direct or indirect contact between firms. However, the concept is not well defined (see Whish, 2003). In the USA the phrase 'express communication' has been mentioned as a possible criterion. As explained in Kaplow and Shapiro (2007), neither this concept is well defined: '*What all of these court decisions and most other statements have in common is that key terms are not defined, the subject is*

Semicollusion can be seen as a version of the broad concept collusion. If there are more than one choice variable, then there are many possible outcomes. They can collude on all choice variables, and this is what we could call collusion. If they compete on some choice variables, this is labeled competition. But if they compete on all choice variables and collude on the other ones, we label it semicollusion.

To our knowledge, the notion semicollusion is rather new in economic literature. Fershtman and Muller (1986) analyze the behavior of firms in what they phrase *"semicollusive"* markets, defined as *"rivals compet[ing] in one variable (or set of variables) and collude in another"*. The decade that followed we saw several contributions to the theoretical literature on semicollusion, and the main contribution until the mid-1990s are surveyed in Chapters 9 and 10 in Phlips (1995).

Despite the rather new interest in the literature on semicollusion, there is no doubt that the phenomenon has been present in numerous industries. Economists have understood this for a long time. They have also described the mechanisms at work, although without using the phrase semicollusion. For example, Fershtman and Muller (1986) refer to Scherer (1970) — where the notion semicollusion is not present — for motivating their modeling approach.

In many theoretical models on collusion, we observe a discussion of more than one variable. We distinguish our survey from a more general survey of collusion by only considering studies where firms by definition have more than one endogenous choice variable.

## 2.2  Anecdotal Evidence

There are numerous anecdotal examples of the existence of semicollusion in specific industries.[3] One example is the coal industry in Germany in the 1920s. In 1919 a legal cartel was formed, where the members agreed on total production and thereby colluded on prices. However, they did not collude on capacities. As described in Bloch

---

*not directly discussed in any depth (that is, for more than a paragraph), and no rationale is offered for deeming on set of scenarios to be legal and another illegal'* (p. 1124).
[3] See, for example, Scherer and Ross (1990), p. 295 and 674.

(1932), the rule for allocating production to each firm led to overinvestment in capacity:

> '*At certain intervals the productive capacity of each individual member firm was determined by expert technologists. The actual production volume was then fixed as a percentage of the productive capacity, this percentage serving at the same time as a basis for allotting votes in the general assembly of the syndicate. The result of this practice was that all members of the syndicate made great efforts to increase their productive capacity in order to have as high a proportional share of the total production as possible assigned to them. Eventually the productive capacity was around 25 per cent above the maximum production during the boom.*' (p. 217).

According to Bloch (1932), a similar pattern emerged in the iron industry in Germany in the 1920s:

> '*Here, too, the cartels, the regulated prices, and the fixing of production quotas in percentages of a technical productive capacity have led to an expansion of the productive capacity far beyond need.*' (p. 220).

Bloch reports other instances as well, and concludes that the German experience in the decade after World War I was price cartels that led to overinvestment in capacities (see Bloch, 1932, p, 221). Phlips (1995) reports on a similar development in the European market for cement and nitrogen fertilizers in the 1920s and refers to this as examples of semicollusion.[4]

Lorange (1973) describes the problems facing the three Norwegian cement producers in the 1960s. They had a price cartel in the domestic market since 1927, and each producer received a share of the domestic market according to its share of total domestic capacity.[5] This led,

---

[4] See Phlips (1962), pp. 152–153, where he also refers to Sections 9 and 10 in Phlips (1962) for further details.

[5] For details concerning this sharing rule, see Steen and Sørgard (1999) and Röller and Steen (2006).

in a similar way as described above, to a race for building capacities. He reports from the renegotiation of the cartel agreement in the early 1960s:

> *'During the opening round for negotiation for a new cartel agreement there appeared to be much dissatisfaction with the apparent lack of industry coordination when it came to capacity expansion. It consequently did not take the parties long to see large potential benefits from a full merger.'* (p. 33)

Scherer (1970) undertakes an overall appraisal of market structure and performance and attributes losses in the order of 0.6% of GNP due to 'excess and inefficient capacity due to industrial cartelization and the stimulus of collusive profits'. In his reasoning about why this is happening he is stating:

> *'Second, and probably more important, collusive agreements which succeed in holding price above cost encourage investment in excess capacity in participants' sales depend in any way upon the amount of capacity they possess. This has been a serious problem in Europe, where antitrust sanctions against cartelization were nonexistent until recently, and where cartels often operated by assigning members output quotas proportional to capacity.'* (p. 407).

Collusion on prices can also affect other choice variables than capacities. For example, it has been argued that the ban on TV advertising for tobacco in 1970 in the USA led to higher profits for the firms (see Eckard, 1991). This can be interpreted as if price collusion triggered tough competition on advertising to capture market shares. A ban then helped the firms to escape from such a costly battle for market shares through investment in advertising on TV. This is in line with the findings concerning the effects of dividing American Tobacco into three separate units in 1911. The federal government won a Sherman Act case against American Tobacco, and the restructuring was supposed to lead to tougher competition. However, according to Tennant (1950) the restructuring triggered a battle for market shares rather than price competition.

In the shipping industry, it is also scope for semicollusion. They have a long tradition for having cooperative agreements between firms, with an exemption for the general ban on price fixing in competition law.[6] For example, in ocean liner shipping they form cartels — denoted conferences — for almost all major international routes. According to Fox (1994), they collude on prices and compete along other dimensions:

> *'Member firms generally charge the conference rate and engage in non-price competition with fellow conference members. Frequency of departures, duration of voyages, and size of ship are common examples of this type of competition'.* (p. 345).

This is the case for liner shipping. As documented in Deltas et al. (1999), in the shipping industry in general there are examples also of not only markets with semicollusion, but also markets with full collusion (where they collude along several dimensions).

On the other hand, there are also instances where firms collude on other choice variables than prices. One prominent example is collusion on R&D. This is quite common among firms. In fact, in most countries competition law allows for collusion on R&D while collusion on prices is banned. For example, they form research joint ventures where they can share information about R&D. There are also examples where they collude on advertising and even are encouraged to do so by the government. In the USA, for example, advertising for milk products is cooperatively managed and this is achieved through mandatory contributions.[7]

As the previous examples indicate, collusion on prices might trigger tougher competition along other choice variables. When they collude on non-price variables, it is not so obvious from the examples that this

---

[6] For example, liner shipping companies have had a block exemption from the general ban on price fixing in Article 81 in the EC Treaty. In October 2008 this exemption was withdrawn.

[7] This example is described in Blisard (1999). For other examples on collusion on non-price variables, see Lande and Marvel (2000).

triggers tougher competition along other choice variables. To the contrary, it has been questioned whether collusion on a non-price variable might trigger collusion on prices. This is a question we will explore in detail.

## 2.3 The Rules of the Game

As the examples in the previous section suggest, there are many alternatives concerning what firms can collude on. As will be clear in the next section, it is decisive for the outcome of semicollusion which choice variable they collude on. In addition, the sequence of moves is also important for the outcome.

Possible choice variables for firms are many, and they include prices, capacities, R&D, location, and advertising. Concerning the rules of the game, it is natural to consider how flexible the various choice variables are. If a choice variable is not flexible — cannot easily be adjusted — it implies that a firm can commit to a specific choice for this variable for a longer period. For example, let us assume that a firm can build a plant at one point in time and that it is not possible to adjust the size of the plant later on. Then the decision to build a plant, which can be considered as capacity, is not flexible. On the other hand, when this firm sells what it produces it can very easily change the price of its product. Then price is a flexible choice variable. This has implications for the sequence of moves. If we assume that capacity is set before price is set, then we implicitly assume that a firm can commit to capacity but not necessarily commit to a specific price.

More generally, prices are typically more flexible and observable than most other choice variables. In line with what we have explained, this makes the following sequence of moves a natural one:

- *Stage 1: Firms set non-price choice variables*
- *Stage 2: Firms set prices*

This is the sequence of moves that is chosen in most models we will refer to in what follows.

The next question is which choice variable firms collude on. In theory of collusion it is typically assumed that they collude on all choice

PRICE

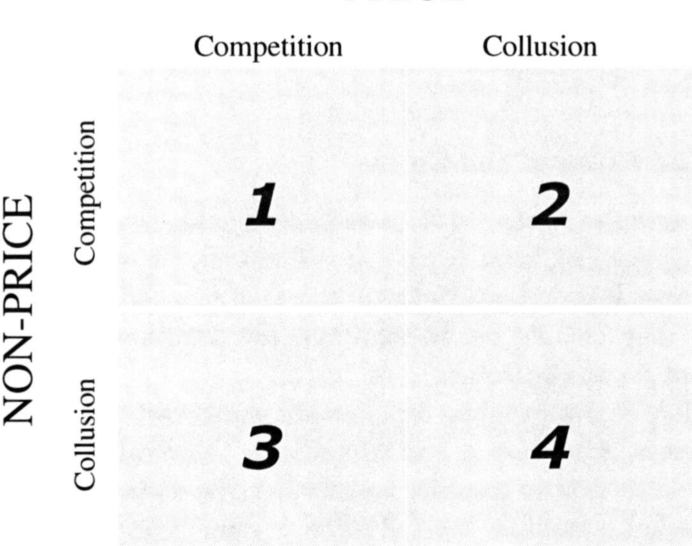

Fig. 2.1  What to collude on?

variables. This is in Figure 2.1 identical to Outcome no. 4, and typically this outcome is compared to Outcome no. 1 which is the competitive outcome.

As should be clear from the previous section, firms in various industries do have colluded on various choice variables and at the same time competed on other choice variables. There are arguments for various combinations of collusion and competition.

First, there are theoretical arguments for collusion on prices. As argued, price is a flexible choice variable. Moreover, prices are often easier to observe than other choice variables such as the amount of R&D or the amount of advertising expenditures. It is well known from theory that if firms can react quickly to any deviation from a collusive outcome this tends to promote collusion. Since prices are flexible and observable, it is possible to (1) observe and (2) react quickly when a rival deviates from price collusion. This suggests that firms collude on prices, and at the same time they might compete on other choice variables. Outcome no. 2 in Figure 2.1 represents such a semicollusive outcome. We are especially concerned about how such an outcome would be compared to a competitive outcome, i.e., outcome no. 1 versus outcome no. 2 in Figure 2.1. In Section 3.2 we discuss in detail various theoretical models where this is the case, and in Section 4.1 we discuss empirical studies that might support the prevalence of such a type of price collusion.

Second, there are arguments against collusion on prices. In most countries' competition law price fixing is illegal. Firms are not allowed to contact each other in order to coordinate prices. On the other hand, competition authorities are much more favorable toward cooperation on other choice variables. For example, European Commission has exempted cooperation on R&D from the general ban on agreements between competing firms.[8] While price fixing is regarded as a hard core cartel, R&D cooperation will in many instances be allowed. This is an argument for observing Outcome no. 3 in Figure 2.1, with collusion on R&D and competition on prices. Collusion on non-price variables — and in particular R&D — are discussed in Sections 3.3 (theory) and 4.2 (empirical findings). As is the case for collusion on prices, the starting point is the comparison between the semicollusive and the competitive outcome, i.e., Outcome nos. 3 and 1 in Figure 2.1. However, a natural question is whether collusion on non-price variables also leads to collusion on prices. Therefore, we also compare Outcome no. 1 and no. 4 versus Outcome no. 1 and no. 3.

---

[8] See Commission regulation No. 2659/2000. According to article 1, firms are allowed to cooperate on research and development, given certain conditions — among other a market share threshold — are met. See Martin (2001), Chapter 5, for a discussion of the competition rules in Europe concerning R&D.

# 3

## Theory of Semicollusion

In this section, we will consider in detail the mechanism at work in an industry where firms collude on one choice variable and compete on other choice variables. Stigler (1968) provided an early contribution to the understanding of the basic mechanism at work.

> *'When a uniform price is agreed upon, or agreed to by, an industry, some or all of the other terms of the sale are left unregulated. [. . . I]n the absence of free entry [..] the question arises: Will any monopoly profit achieved by suppressing price competition be eliminated by non-price competition?'*

What we will discuss under and can learn from the literature on semicollusion is that Stigler's question can have a somewhat surprising answer: Firms can be better off not colluding in a setting of semicollusion, and in some cases consumers are even worse off from semicollusion than outright monopolization. However, it turns out that this is not a general result. Depending on which choice variable they collude on, firms as well as consumers can be either better or worse off. We have to look into the details of the game to find out whether firms, consumers, and the society benefit from semicollusion. This is what we will discuss in the following by a survey of theoretical studies in this section and a survey of empirical studies in the next section.

## 3.1   A Preliminary

To get a first understanding of the possible mechanism at work, let us consider a simple setting. We assume that firms set advertising level and earn revenues from having a positive price–cost margin. Following Schmalensee (1994), we define firm $i$'s profit as follows:

$$\pi_i = (P - C)S \left( \frac{A_i^e}{\sum_{j=1}^{N} A_j^e} \right) - A_i - \sigma \tag{3.1}$$

where $P$ and $C$ denote price and marginal cost, respectively, assuming symmetric firms. $S$ is a proxy for market size, $A_i$ denotes advertising level for firm $i$, and $\sigma$ entry costs for each firm. The parameter $e$, where $0 \leq e \leq 2$, captures own sales' response to own advertising; the higher the $e$, the larger the effect on own sales to own advertising. By assumption, each firm's sale is determined by its share of total advertising outlays in the industry. Such a sharing rule can be observed in numerous cartels.[1] It can also be derived from the notion of fairness presented in Rawls (1971).[2]

Each firm sets an optimal level of advertising. From firm $i$'s first-order condition we have that the advertising level chosen by firm $i$ is the following:

$$A_i = \left[ \frac{1}{N} - \frac{1}{N^2} \right] [e(P - C)S] \tag{3.2}$$

In line with what we expect, each firm's advertising is increasing in market size and decreasing in the number of firms in the industry. More

---

[1] See, for example, the examples in Borch (1932) concerning cartels in Germany. Vasconcelos (2005), employing this rule in his model, refers to several other cartels that used this sharing rule.

[2] In Bos and Harrington, Jr. (2010), Appendix A, this is proven.

importantly for our purpose, we observe that each firm's advertising is increasing in its price–cost margin.

Although we have not modeled the price setting as such, the relationship between the price–cost margin and the amount of advertising captures a main mechanism in many (but not all) semicollusive models. A high price–cost margin will, by definition, imply that the revenues from one additional sold unit are high. Since each firm earns more revenues from an extra unit sold, each firm will spend more resources on sales generating activities. In this case, it implies that a higher price–cost margin triggers more advertising. In other cases this might lead to, say, more R&D. By dampening competition on prices, this might trigger tougher competition along other dimensions. In what follows we will look more carefully into this mechanism, to see whether this result is robust.

## 3.2 Collusion on Prices

In theoretical models the most common choice variable to collude on is prices. This is already indicated in the previous section, where we briefly discussed how higher prices would affect another choice variable (in that case advertising). In what follows we go through some of the models in the literature on collusion on prices and competition along other dimensions.

### 3.2.1 Competition on Capacities

There are several papers analyzing the market outcome when firms compete on capacities and collude on prices. We start out by a very simple model that was introduced in Fershtman and Gandal (1994). Later on, we refer to other models that can be regarded as extensions of the Fershtman/Gandal model.

#### 3.2.1.1 A Basic Model

Let us consider the modeling approach in Fershtman and Gandal (1994).[3] It is a duopoly where firms choose capacities in the first stage

---

[3] Brander and Harris (1984) consider a quite similar setting, where the profit in the semicollusive outcome is divided in proportion to the capacities of the firm.

and prices in the second stage. There is a technology with zero marginal costs and the cost of installing capacity $k_i$ for firm $i$ is $C(k_i) = \gamma_i$. Firms produce identical products, and the market demand is given by the linear demand function $D(p) = 1 - p$. They assume efficient rationing, which implies that they can apply the result first shown in Kreps and Scheinkman (1983) for the alternative with competition on both capacities and prices.

The first alternative is competition on both stages. As first shown in Kreps and Scheinkman (1983), this will lead to a Cournot outcome. It implies that the equilibrium outcome is identical to the one where firms set quantities and marginal cost of production is $\gamma$. They use all their installed capacity for production. If we let $q_i$ denote production of firm $i$, then the equilibrium capacity and production is as follows for firm $i$ (where superscript $N$ denotes competition at both stages):

$$k_i^N = q_i^N = \frac{1 - \gamma}{3}. \tag{3.3}$$

And the corresponding profits for each firm:

$$\pi_i^N = \frac{(1 - \gamma)^2}{9}. \tag{3.4}$$

They assume that $\gamma < 1/4$, which ensures that the price, $p = (1 + 2\gamma)/3$, is below the second-stage monopoly price.

This alternative is compared with the case where the firms compete on capacities at Stage 1 and collude on prices at Stage 2. If no capacity constraints, the price is set equal to $1/2$, the monopoly price at zero marginal cost, and total quantity sold is $1/2$. This means that as long as $k_1 + k_2 \geq 1/2$, the collusive price is assumed to be $1/2$. If $k_1 + k_2 < 1/2$, the capacities are binding and the price is $1 - (k_1 + k_2) > 1/2$.

If $k_1 + k_2 > 1/2$, total capacity exceeds total production (which is equal to $1/2$). There are various ways to allocate total production between firms. Fershtman and Gandal (1994) assume that if total production exceeds sales at the collusive price, production is allocated according to relative capacity. As argued above, this sharing rule is in accordance with what we observe in many industries and can also be derived from the definition of fairness in Rawls (1971). Formally, such a sharing rule is as follows (with superscript $C$ for collusion on prices):

$$q_i^C = \frac{k_i}{k_i + k_j}.$$ (3.5)

Given such an allocation rule, firm $i$ has the following profit at Stage 1:

$$\pi_i(k_i, k_j) = \begin{cases} k_i(1 - k_i - k_j) - \gamma k_i & \textit{if } k_i + k_j < 1/2 \\ \frac{k_i}{k_i+k_j}\frac{1}{4} - \gamma k_i & \textit{if } k_i + k_j \geq 1/2 \end{cases}.$$ (3.6)

Under the assumptions we have made, $k_1 + k_2 < 1/2$ cannot be an equilibrium.[4] From the first-order condition for the case where $k_1 + k_2 \geq 1/2$, we find that the capacity for firm $i$ is the following:

$$k_i^C = \frac{1}{16\gamma}.$$ (3.7)

As shown in Fershtman and Gandal (1994), a unilateral deviation is not profitable and therefore this is the equilibrium capacities if they compete on capacities at Stage 1 and collude on prices at Stage 2.

Given that $\gamma < 1/4$, we see that each firm's capacity always exceeds $1/4$. Since a collusive price of $1/2$ implies that each of them produces $1/4$, then both firms carries excess capacity in the semicollusive equilibrium.

Now we can compare the equilibrium capacities, production, and prices for semicollusion with the scenario where they compete on both capacities and prices. First, note that prices are higher with semicollusion. This is no surprise, since they collude on prices in the semicollusive regime and by assumption are able to set the monopoly price at Stage 2. Consistent with such prices, we observe that total production is lower with semicollusion than with competition. However, the excess capacity with semicollusion is such that total capacity is larger with semicollusion than with competition. It implies that there are costs of installing capacity associated with a semicollusive outcome. We have the following profits for firm $i$ with semicollusion:

$$\pi_i^C = q_i^C \cdot p^m - \gamma k_i = \frac{1}{16}.$$ (3.8)

---

[4] In such an outcome the prices in the Cournot game exceeds $1/2$, which contradicts the assumption that $\gamma < 1/4$ whereby Cournot prices are below $1/2$.

When comparing with the profits if competition at both stages, it can easily be verified that each firm earns higher profits if they do not collude on prices.

This is a counterintuitive result. By coordinating prices, they earn lower profits even though they succeed in setting higher prices. The driving force is exactly the mechanism we described in Section 3.1. A higher price triggers more intense rivalry along other dimensions, because the profit from capturing one more customer is higher than before. In this particular case there is a battle for market shares through the installment of capacity. The installment of capacity is costly. In the simple model in Fershtman and Gandal (1994) it is found that the cost associated with installment of capacity not used for production more than outweighs the increase in revenues from colluding on prices.

### 3.2.1.2    Extensions of the Basic Model

There are numerous simplifying assumptions in the basic model we have referred to. There are several extensions of the basic model, and interestingly many of them are introduced in studies that were completed prior to Fershtman and Gandal's (1994) study.

First, there is reason to questioning the sharing rule as such. In the basic model it was simply assumed that if excess capacity in the industry due to collusive pricing they allocated production according to relative capacity. Osborne and Pitchik (1987) relax this assumption. In line with our basic model, they assume that firms set capacities non-cooperatively at Stage 1 and that they anticipate that they might collude on prices at Stage 2. In contrast to our basic model, each firm's quota is determined by its threat to deviate from the collusive price at Stage 2.[5] It turns out that in line with what we found in our basic model, the firms end up installing more capacity than what is needed for production. They install excess capacity, because it helps as a threat toward the other cartels members concerning what will happen

---

[5] There are several ways the quota can be set, see Schmalensee (1987). In Osborne and Pitchik (1987) they apply the Nash bargaining solution, where the firms split equally the excess of monopoly profit over the payoffs when the threats are carried out. It is assumed that there will be a non-cooperative price-setting game if the threats are carried out.

at Stage 2 (a one shot game) if this firm deviates from the collusive price.

One important implication from the Osborne and Pitchik (1987) model is that the small firm — the one with the lowest capacity — can be the one with the highest profits per unit of capacity. To understand this, note that for sufficiently large capacity by both firms they will both be able to credible threat to flood the market. This implies that they split equally the gain from price collusion at Stage 2. But if one of the firms has a lower capacity than the other one, the firm with the lowest capacity has the highest profit per unit of capacity.

Second, there is also reason to question whether price collusion is indeed the outcome at Stage 2 of the game. Davidson and Deneckere (1990) relax this assumption.[6] While at Stage 1 capacity is set non-cooperatively in their model as well, they assume that at Stage 2 of the game the firms play an infinitely repeated price-setting game. They find that excess capacity is present in all outcomes (except for the static Nash equilibrium in quantities). Excess capacity makes it possible to punish a deviation from a collusive scheme. If the costs of capital and the interest rate are sufficiently low, then an equilibrium with high excess capacity and a monopoly price is sustainable. If the cost of capital and the interest rate rise, it is costly to carry a large excess capacity. Then the collusive price falls below the monopoly price.

Note that also in this model there is a capacity 'race', because each firm tries to increase its share of the collusive profit. In that respect there are some similarities with our basic model. While in our basic model the mechanism that led to excess capacity followed directly from the way they set the quota (the market sharing rule they had agreed upon), it is a more indirect mechanism in the repeated game.

A semicollusive approach can also be relevant in entry games. Firms set capacities non-cooperatively prior to entry, and then there are prospects for collusion on prices after entry. In Benoit and Krishna (1991) an incumbent and an entrant set capacities sequentially before

---

[6] They extend a model first introduced in Davidson and Deneckere (1984) and Benoit and Krishna (1987). In both those models firms are allowed to collude on both prices and capacities. See also Fershtman and Muller (1986), the first one to show that semicollusion might lead to excess capacity.

an infinitely repeated price game after entry. Given the prospects for collusion after entry, a high capacity by the incumbent might signal a large scope for collusion. This implies that a large investment in capacities by the incumbent might accommodate entry. Benoit and Krishna (1991) show that a limited capacity can in some cases deter entry, because it makes it credible that collusion is not attainable.[7]

### 3.2.1.3   Profits and Welfare

A semicollusive behavior will obviously have an impact on profits. As noted by Davidson and Deneckere (1990), equilibrium profit in a semicollusive outcome is expected to be lower than in a fully collusive outcome. The reason is that semicollusion leads to an expansion of capacity beyond the monopoly level. Obviously, this expansion is costly. As shown in Fershtman and Gandal (1994), the profit increase due to higher prices can be outweighed by the cost increase due to the expansion of capacity.

A natural question then is whether a semicollusive outcome will be achieved, given that they are worse off than in a competitive outcome. Note that firms collude at Stage 2. For a given capacity, it will always be profitable for the firms to collude on prices at Stage 2 (as long as such an outcome is sustainable in the repeated game). This implies that it can be difficult to deviate from a semicollusive outcome. It will not be credible to agree on not colluding on prices unless such an agreement is a commitment for the firms.

The mechanism so far may indicate that semicollusion leads to lower welfare. This can be explained from Figure 3.1.

Following Fershtman and Gandal (1994), we assume that competition on both capacities and prices leads to a Cournot outcome. They install total capacity $K^N$, which is above the total capacity chosen by a monopoly firm $K^M$. If collusion on prices, they are able to reach the monopoly price $P^M$, which is above the Cournot price $P^N$. Compared to the case of competition at both stages, this leads to a dead weight loss shown with the area marked with the dark gray color. Collusion

---

[7] See also Sørgard (1997), where it is shown that an entrant facing an incumbent with excess capacity might support post entry price collusion by restricting its own capacity.

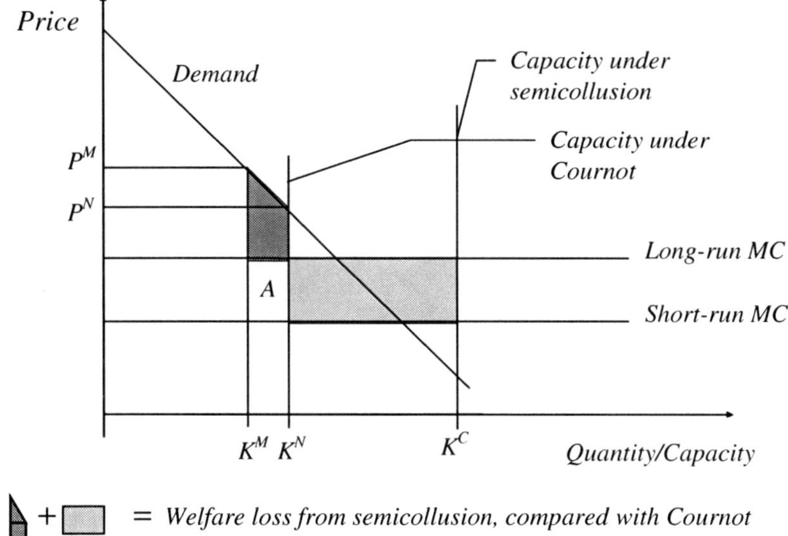


Fig. 3.1 Possible welfare effects of collusion on prices and competition on capacities.

on prices and competition on capacities will lead to an installment of capacity equal to $K^C$, which is in excess the amount of capacity if competition on prices. This is costly for the firms and for society, and it leads to an additional loss for society equal to the rectangular area marked with a light gray color. The total costs for society associated with semicollusion are the sum of the areas that are marked with colors.

In fact, in this setting a semicollusive outcome is even worse than a fully collusive outcome. If a fully collusive outcome, they don't install excess capacity. The only costs for society are then the dead weight loss associated with high prices, shown with the area marked with a dark gray color. The additional loss associated with installing excess capacity with semicollusion is the light gray rectangle plus the rectangle marked with an $A$.

### 3.2.2   Competition on R&D

In the previous section the firm had prices and capacities as choice variables. An alternative could be that they can set prices and R&D. For example, R&D can lead to lower costs of production (lower marginal costs). If so, this is process innovation. Alternatively, R&D leads to product innovation and thereby product improvements.

### 3.2.2.1  A Basic Model

Let us consider the model first presented in Fershtman and Gandal (1994). They assume a market with two firms producing identical products and with a linear demand:

$$P = 1 - q_1 - q_2, \tag{3.9}$$

where $P$ denotes the market price and $q_i$ denotes the production (and sales) of firm $i$. Each firm's costs are determined by its investment in R&D:

$$C_i = (A - x_i)q_i + \lambda x_i^2/2, \tag{3.10}$$

where $x_i$ denotes firm $i$'s investment in R&D, where $x_i \leq A$. The first term is the cost of production, while the second term is the investment cost.

The rules of the games are as follows:

- Stage 1: firms set R&D $(x_i)$
- Stage 2: Firms set quantities $(q_i)$

In the first scenario, called competition, they set both R&D and quantities non-cooperatively. In the second scenario they set R&D non-cooperatively at Stage 1 and collude on quantities at Stage 2.

If competition, they behave a la Cournot at Stage 2. The second-stage profits of firm $i$ net of investment are as follows:

$$R_i^N = \frac{(1 - A + 2x_i - x_j)^2}{9}. \tag{3.11}$$

Assuming an interior solution, the unique equilibrium level of R&D for each firm is[8]

$$x_i^N = \frac{4(1 - A)}{9\lambda - 4}, \tag{3.12}$$

---

[8] To ensure an interior solution in both competition and semicollusion scenarios, it is assumed that $\lambda < 9/8$ and $\lambda^* A > 1/2 \geq A$. For details, see Fershtman and Gandal (1994).

and the corresponding profit is:

$$\pi_i^N = \frac{\lambda(1-A)^2(9\lambda - 8)}{(9\lambda - 4)^2}. \tag{3.13}$$

This scenario with competition is contrasted with the scenario with semicollusion. Assuming semicollusion, it is important how the firms divide the sales in the collusive outcome at Stage 2. Fershtman and Gandal assume that the firms sign a binding agreement, where $s_i$ denotes the share of the total sales given to firm $i$. Then the sales of firm $i$ is $q_i = s_i(1 - P)$, which implies that the second-period profits for firm $i$ net of investment are as follows:

$$R_i^C = \frac{(1 - A + x_i)^2 \cdot s_i}{4}. \tag{3.14}$$

Fershtman and Gandal assume that $s_i$ is set such that firms receive equal percentage gains over the profits that would be earned in the competition scenario. Given investments at Stage 2, $s_1$, and $s_2$ are set such that:

$$\frac{R_1^C(x_1, x_2)}{R_1^N(x_1, x_2)} = \frac{R_2^C(x_1, x_2)}{R_2^N(x_1, x_2)}. \tag{3.15}$$

Setting $s_2 = 1 - s_1$ and substituting (3.11) and (3.14) into (3.15), we have the formula for how firm 1's share is determined:

$$s_1 = \frac{(1 - A + x_2)^2 \cdot (1 - A + 2x_1 - x_2)^2}{(1 - A + x_2)^2 \cdot (1 - A + 2x_1 - x_2)^2 + M}, \tag{3.16}$$

where $M = (1 - A + x_1)^2 \cdot (1 - A + 2x_2 - x_1)^2$. Given such a sharing rule, the equilibrium levels of R&D and profits are as follows:

$$x_i^C = \frac{(1 - A)}{2\lambda - 1}, \tag{3.17}$$

$$\pi_i^C = \frac{\lambda(1 - A)^2(\lambda - 1)}{2(2\lambda - 1)^2}. \tag{3.18}$$

It can now easily be verified that $x_i^C > x_i^N$. This implies that firms invest more in R&D when they collude at Stage 2 than if they compete at Stage 2. The basic mechanism is analogous to the one we described in the previous section. Firms invest heavily at Stage 1 in order to capture a larger share of the collusive profits at Stage 2.

It can also be shown that if investment costs are sufficiently small (low $\lambda$), semicollusion leads to lower profits than competition. For low costs of investing in R&D, the firms invests a large amount at Stage 1 in order to have a larger share of the collusive profit that is generated at Stage 2. The gain from a collusive price is then outweighed by cost associated with large costs of investment in R&D. This is similar to what we found in the case of semicollusion on capacity.

### 3.2.2.2 Extensions of the Basic Model

As should be clear from the previous section, there are some similarities in structure between collusion on capacities and collusion on R&D. But let us first focus on one feature that is distinctly different when they choose R&D instead or capacities. It is well known that R&D can lead to spillovers, i.e., transmission of useful technological information from one firm to others. One argument could be that information is spread through the mobility of workers between firms in the same industry.

Brod and Shivakumar (1999) have extended the Fershtman and Gandal model to the case with technological spillovers. Firm $i$'s cost function is the following:

$$C_i = (c - x_i - \beta x_j)q_i + \lambda x_i^2/2. \tag{3.19}$$

If $\beta = 0$, there is no technological spillovers and we have a model that in this respect is identical to Fershtman and Gandal. Brod and Shivakumar assume non-negative spillovers by assuming that $0 \leq \beta \leq 1$, where $\beta = 1$ implies perfect spillovers.

In addition, Brod and Shivakumar have employed a demand system that differs from Fershtman and Gandal by assuming that:

$$P_i = A - b(q_i + \gamma q_j). \tag{3.20}$$

The model in Fershtman and Gandal is a special case, where $A = b = \gamma = 1$.

There is one more important difference between those two models. While Fershtman and Gandal use a market sharing device (see above), there are no side payments in Brod and Shivakumar. Each firm produces what is demanded of its own product at Stage 2. The prices are set such that the firm's total profits are maximized, i.e., as if prices are set by a multiproduct monopoly firm. Such a mechanism for allocating sales implies that their model is not valid for the case of identical products ($\gamma = 1$), since in that case one needs a mechanism for allocating production between the firms.

It turns out that the results concerning investment in R&D are in line with the results found in Fershtman and Gandal. For all feasible levels of spillovers ($0 \leq \beta \leq 1$) and differentiation ($0 \leq \gamma < 1$), investment in R&D is higher in the scenario with semicollusion than the scenario with competition. This is explained as follows:

> *'One might have expected the opposite of Proposition 1 [more R&D if competition], because R&D is an output-enhancing activity, and firms that collude downstream tend to restrict output. Indeed, firms colluding downstream do restrict output for a given R&D effort. But each cartel member's output share depends on its marginal cost, which in turn depends on its R&D effort. The higher price–cost margins earned by the cartel induce its members to value R&D more highly than they would under downstream competition.'* (p. 226).

This illustrates that an analogous mechanism is present in this model as in Fershtman and Gandal, despite the lack of any formal market sharing agreement. The mechanism is not identical, though. The increase in the price–cost margin is in this case partly caused by lower marginal costs, which in turn triggers more investments in R&D.

Note that the price setting at Stage 2 can be seen as a formal agreement between the firms. They agree on setting prices that maximize joint profits, and then each firm sells exact the amount that is demanded for its own product at those prices. The latter is the main difference from Fershtman and Gandal, where a mechanism was introduced that allocated production when all firms produced an identical product.

Brod and Shivakumar show how results concerning profits may change when spillovers and product differentiation are introduced. They find that if the products are differentiated, then semicollusion is profitable if spillovers are sufficiently large. The reason is straightforward. Spillovers implies that the gain associated with an investment in R&D spills over to other firms in the industry, and then they are jointly better off when semicollusion triggers more investment in R&D.

Mukherjee (2002) has chosen an alternative method for modeling R&D. In contrast to those two works described above, he assumes that the success of R&D is uncertain. If the probability of success is low, denoted low R&D productivity, it will increase the probability that the firm is the sole innovator. Assuming drastic innovation, it implies that the firm that succeeds gains a monopoly position. He finds that for low R&D productivity, the investment in R&D can be lower in a semicollusive regime than a regime where they compete on quantities at Stage 2.

All of the studies we have referred so far have simply assumed that firms compete on R&D at Stage 1 and collude on prices at Stage 2. In contrast, Fershtman and Pakes (2000) analyze whether a collusive outcome is sustainable, i.e., whether firms find it individual rational to collude on prices at Stage 2. Building on the framework first introduced in Ericson and Pakes (1995), they use numerical methods in a dynamic model with entry and exit. They assume that firms invest in product innovation at Stage 1. If a firm deviates from a collusive price, all firms revert to playing static Nash equilibrium. It is found that collusion on prices is hard to sustain if a firm is likely to exit in the near future. Note that this study is, as far as we know, the only one that considers semicollusion where they compete on product innovation.

### 3.2.2.3  Welfare Considerations

We found that semicollusion on capacities leads to not only a dead weight loss, but also costs associated with the installment of excess capacity. However, the establishment of collusion on R&D but not on prices has an ambiguous effect on welfare. On one hand, prices might increase following collusion at Stage 2. On the other hand, costs might go down due to lower marginal costs following investment in R&D if process innovation. The latter can even reverse the price effect, since for a sufficiently large reduction in marginal costs prices are lower with semicollusion than with competition. Even if prices go up, improvement in products due to product innovation can outweigh the loss for the consumers of a higher price.

Fershtman and Gandal found that in their setting there is no scope for lower prices following semicollusion, despite the fact that semicollusion leads to lower marginal costs. A more general setting is analyzed in Matsui (1989), motivated by the government-supported formation of cartels in Japan after World War II. He shows that investment that leads to lower marginal costs might lead to benefits to consumers. This is the case if the reduction in marginal costs outweighs the firm's incentives to raise prices following the establishment of semicollusion. Note, however, that even if consumers benefit from semicollusion it can be detrimental to total welfare. This is easily seen if we consider the case where semicollusion leads to no changes in prices and thereby consumers are unaffected by it. Welfare has dropped if total costs have increased. Semicollusion leads to more investments, but on the other hand lower marginal costs. If this was profitable for each firm prior to semicollusion, it would choose to invest also then. But if this investment is undertaken only after semicollusion is in place, it implies that total costs have increased and welfare is reduced.

In Fershtman and Pakes (2000) R&D leads to higher quality on products (product innovation). Collusion on prices leads to more investments in product innovation. This leads to better products, but also to higher prices. Using numerical simulations they find that consumers are better off; the product improvement outweighs the price increase. In some cases collusion is beneficial for consumers since the quality of the product is improved when they don't compete on prices. They therefore conclude that there is a need to revise the common attitude toward collusion, although they admit that the modeling is incomplete.

### 3.2.3 Competition on Location

In the previous section we assumed implicitly that firms produced identical products. Often differentiation is a choice variable. Differentiation can be either in space, or more general in product attributes. In what follows we concentrate on differentiation in space by discussing models where firms choose location. In addition, we also briefly refer to studies of product differentiation more in general and how it affects collusion on prices.

### 3.2.3.1  A Basic Model

A common modeling approach of differentiation can be traced back to Hotelling (1929). He introduced a duopoly model for location on a straight line. His simple model can be illustrated in Figure 3.2.

Consumers are located on a straight line, illustrated with the line from zero to one in Figure 3.2. Firms $A$ and $B$ choose location on the straight line, and their locations are illustrated with locations denoted $A$ and $B$ in Figure 3.2. If firms set identical prices, each consumer will then go to the closest firm. They will then incur a transportation cost that corresponds to the length of transportation. For example, a consumer located at zero would prefer firm A and incur a transportation cost for the distance $a$. According to Hotelling (1929), competing firms would locate close to each other (identical location — minimum differentiation). In Figure 3.2 this would imply that both firms locate at 1/2.

Unfortunately, his analysis was incomplete. Given competition on both prices and location, identical location would not be an equilibrium outcome in pure strategies.[9] For example, with quadratic transportation costs and competition along both dimensions firms choose maximum differentiation (locate on zero and one on the straight line, respectively). This is done for dampening price competition. If we allow

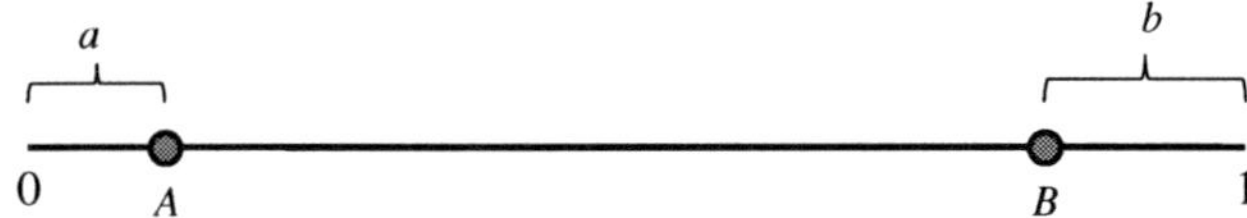


Fig. 3.2 Hotelling location model.

---

[9] This was first pointed out in d'Aspremont et al. (1979). The reason is that a firm then could capture all the rival's sale by lowering its price. As shown in Dasgupta and Maskin (1986), the equilibrium is in mixed strategies.

for collusion on both prices and location, that would neither restore the original outcome proposed in Hotelling (1929). By locating at 1/4 and 3/4, respectively, the firms would minimize transportation costs. This would, in turn, lead to higher profits since firms are able to set a higher price to the consumers.

In Friedman and Thisse (1993), it is proposed a game where the Hotelling result of minimum differentiation is restored.[10] They assume that firms at Stage 1 choose location non-cooperatively and at Stage 2 set prices in an infinitely repeated game. They show that a trigger strategy can support an equilibrium outcome with a fully collusive outcome and minimum differentiation.

To have an indication of the mechanisms at work, let us consider the profit function for firm $A$:

$$\pi_A = [P_A(A, B) - C] \cdot D_A(A, B, P_A(A, B), P_B(A, B)). \qquad (3.21)$$

A marginal change in the location of firm $A$ will then have the following effect:

$$\frac{\partial \pi_A}{\partial A} = \underbrace{[P_A - C]\frac{\partial D_A}{\partial A}}_{DIRECT\ EFFECT} + \underbrace{[P_A - C]\frac{\partial D_A}{\partial P_B}\frac{\partial P_B}{\partial A}}_{STRATEGIC\ EFFECT}. \qquad (3.22)$$

All else equal, if firm $A$ moves closer to rival's location (higher $A$) it will have a larger sale. This is because some of the consumers that were located closest to firm $B$ will now be better off by choosing firm $A$. This is the direct effect, and it tells the firm to move closer to its rival. But if it moves closer to its rival, this will trigger tougher competition on prices. The products are becoming closer substitutes, and then it is more tempting to cut prices to capture some of the rival's customers. This is the strategic effect, and this will tell the firm to move away from its rival to dampening competition.

We thus see that location is ambiguous. It depends, among other things, on the transportation costs. However, if the firms collude on prices this will change. In such a case there is no strategic effect, since locating closer to its rival will not trigger any price response (given

---

[10] See also Jèhiel (1992), who reports a similar result and also uses a Hotelling framework. He also shows that if monetary transfers are possible, this may lead to differentiation.

that they succeed in colluding on prices). If so, only the direct effect is present. The firms will then locate close to its rival to capture sales from its rival. As shown in Friedman and Thisse (1993), in the semicollusive equilibrium they locate at the same point and this restores what Hotelling characterized as "excessive sameness".

The robustness of the result in Friedman and Thisse (1993) is even stronger than indicated by the discussion of the direct and strategic effect. They assume that collusion on prices is supported by a trigger strategy, where a firm's profit is proportional to profits at the single-shot equilibrium. It is well known from theory of repeated games that the more severe the punishment after any deviation, the larger the scope for collusion on prices. If they have chosen identical location, the one-shot equilibrium is zero and thus the most severe that is possible. This explains why it is larger scope for collusion on prices when both firms locate at $(1/2, 1/2)$ than, for example, at the end points.

### 3.2.3.2  Extensions of the Basic Model

Friedman and Thisse (1993) consider only two firms, and this is obviously a restrictive assumption. To our knowledge there are no theoretical studies of semicollusion with a similar setting as them with more than two firms. It is not at all obvious that their result would carry through to three or more firms. Although Eaton and Lipsey (1975) do not solve the semicollusive game, their study indicates that things may change dramatically if we have more than two firms.

They assume that prices are exogenously given, while firms compete on location. They solve for various assumptions, for example concerning the number of firms, one or two dimensional product differentiation, whether the location is on a straight line or on a circle, and how customers are spread throughout the market. For the moment, let us stick to the Hotelling model discussed above and only check the effect of the number of firms.[11] The results in Eaton and Lipsey (1975) are illustrated in Figure 3.3.

---

[11] In Eaton and Lipsey (1975) they assume that each firm offers one product. Often we observe that firms offer more than one product. For a discussion of such a case, see

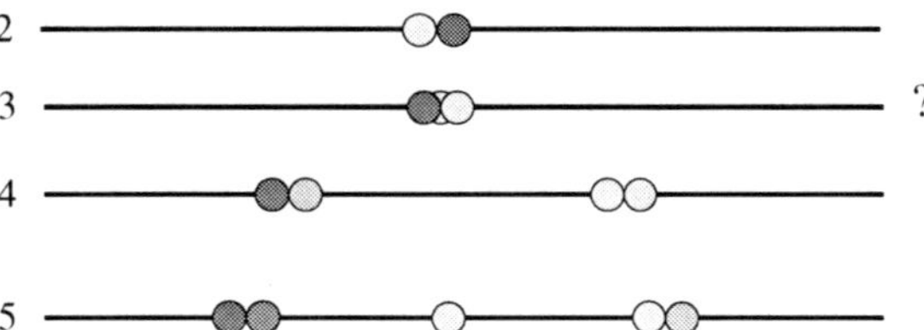

Fig. 3.3 Location with exogenous prices for two to five firms.

For two firms we see that they have chosen minimum differentiation, which is in line with the result in Friedman and Thisse (1993). For three firms, there is no Nash equilibrium in pure strategies. Each of the firms most to the left and right, respectively, would gain from moving toward the third firm, the one located between them. But if they move close enough, the firm in the middle would find it profitable to deviate, and become the firm located most to the left or most to the right. If there are four firms, on the other hand, they locate pairwise as shown in Figure 3.3. If the customers are evenly spread out, the firms are located pairwise at the first and third quartiles.[12] With five firms, pairwise location is no longer possible. They show that in equilibrium firms are located pairwise at 1/6 and 5/6 of the distance of the line, while the last firm is located in the center of the market. Moreover, they also show that location is ambiguous for the case with six or more firms.

This example indicates that the result in Friedman and Thisse (1993) is not robust to changes in the number of firms. Eaton and Lipsey (1975) show that other relaxations of the model may also change the main result found in Friedman and Thisse (1993). For example, they show that if we assume that customers are located on a circle rather than on a line minimum differentiation disappears even for the case of only two firms.

---

Gabszewicz and Thisse (1986), Bensaid and DePalma (1993), and Martinez-Giralt and Neven (1988).

[12] In Gabszewicz and Thisse (1986) it is shown that pairwise location is also the equilibrium outcome in a duopoly where the firms have an equal number of products. However, in Salvanes et al. (1997) it is shown that in a duopoly with an unequal number for products there is no Nash equilibrium in pure strategies. The firm with the largest number of firms would try to squeeze the small one by locating on both sides of it, and the small firm would try to escape from this.

Finally, let us consider models that analyze how product differentiation more generally can influence the prospects for price collusion. As first discussed in Chang (1991) and Ross (1992), there are two opposing effects.[13] If products are close substitutes, a deviating firm can gain a lot because it can capture a large fraction of the rivals' sales. On the other hand, after deviation firms compete fiercely if their products are close substitutes. Depending on the modeling approach and assumptions made, a reduction in product differentiation can either support or destabilize collusion on prices. For example, in contrast to the results in Friedman and Thisse (1993) it is shown in Ross (1992) that in a particular spatial model an increase in product differentiation can promote price collusion. Note, though, that none of the general models on cartel stability and product differentiation treat product differentiation as an endogenous choice variable.

### 3.2.3.3   Profits and Welfare

If we return to the basic model, it is straight forward to see that the two firms are not able to reach the profits they could reach in a fully collusive equilibrium. They could jointly be better off if they located on the first and third quartiles, respectively. That would be more in line with the preferences for the consumers (lower transportation costs), and this would make it possible to charge a higher price. But as we have shown already in the preliminary section, high prices may trigger tougher competition along other dimensions. In this particular case it triggers competition for market shares through a more aggressive behavior concerning location.

In the basic model it is thus straight forward to see, as argued above, that semicollusion leads to lower welfare than the fully collusive outcome. It can also lead to lower welfare than in the competitive outcome. Although location is ambiguous with competition, it can never be more extreme than both locating in the middle and the prices can never be higher than in the semicollusive outcome.

---

[13] The point that cheating will be less profitable when products are differentiated was first discussed in Davidson (1983). See also Rotschild (1997), Tyagi (1999) and Chang (1992).

Unfortunately, these clear cut results do not carry over to the extensions of the basic model. As we have explained, collusion on prices and competition on location can lead to outcomes that differs a lot depending on, for example, how many firms that compete. There is therefore not possible to make any general conclusion concerning the welfare effect of collusion on prices and competition on location. It calls for a case-by-case approach.

### 3.2.4 Competition on Advertising

Advertising is a choice variable in numerous industries. In Section 3.1 we reported a specific model where each firm's advertising was decisive for the market sharing. In that setting there was no market expansion effect following an increase in advertising. Let us introduce an alternative modeling approach to capture the potential for a market expansion effect.

Let us briefly explain the approach presented in Wang et al. (2007). They employ a theoretical model to make predictions they test. In the theoretical model they assume the following linear demand function for product $i$:

$$X_i = (A + y_i - by_j) - p_i + dp_j, \tag{3.23}$$

where $X_i$ is the quantity of product $i$, $p_i$ is the price of product $i$, $y_i$ is the amount of advertising for product $i$, $d$ is a proxy for the degree of product differentiation, and $b$ is a proxy for the spillover. If $b > 0$, then there is a negative spillover; the potential for increased own sale due to own advertising is partial offset by increased sales by the other firm.

Obviously, it can be argued that this is a rather special demand structure. For example, it is assumed that advertising leads to higher willingness to pay (upward shift in the demand curve), not in a larger number of consumers as such. It is also quite clear that the results depend crucially on the parameter values.

There are some results though that indicates that the results we found in previous sections are valid also with collusion on prices and competition on advertising. First, they find that for sufficiently large spillover the amount of advertising is larger in the semicollusive regime than the competition regime. Second, they find that for sufficiently high costs associated with investing in advertising the firms are better off with competition than with semicollusion.

To our knowledge, there are not any other theoretical studies that analyze collusion on prices and competition on advertising. The modeling approach should share some similarities with the approach taken on models with R&D. Both investment in advertising and in R&D can be interpreted as an investment that change the demand for the product in question. This is the approach followed in Symeonidis (2000a), which we will describe later on when we discuss semicollusion with free entry. This implies that some of the results we found from models with R&D can be relevant for the discussion of the effects of collusion on prices and competition on advertising.

## 3.3 Competition on Prices

As argued in Section 2.3, it will often be more plausible with collusion on prices than on other choice variables. The main reason for this is that price is typically a flexible variable that is observable and therefore can be changed quite rapidly, and it is well known that it is easier to collude the more flexible a choice variable is. However, there are in some cases arguments for collusion on other choice variables than prices. In particular, competition law in most countries typically ban any contact between competing firms concerning price fixing. Overt collusion on prices is therefore for most firms not an option unless they decide to take part in an illegal activity. On the other hand, collusive agreements on other choice variables are often legal and such cooperation is in some cases encouraged by the competition authorities. This is in particular true concerning collusion on research and development. For example, European Commission has exempted research and development from the general ban on agreements between undertakings. This makes it very natural to investigate the effects of collusion on R&D combined with competition on prices.

### 3.3.1    Collusion on R&D

#### 3.3.1.1    A Basic Model

Let us consider the model presented in d'Aspremont and Jacquemin (1988). They apply a duopoly model with identical products, linear demand and a quadratic cost function. Let $q_i$ and $x_i$ denote firm $i$'s amount of quantity sold and research undertaken, respectively. The price is given by $p = a - b(q_1 + q_2)$, and the cost function for firm $i$ is $C_i = [A - x_i + \beta x_j]q_i + \gamma x_i^2/2$. They assume that the research activity is set at Stage 1 and the production is set at Stage 2.

In line with the previous section, let us compare the competitive outcome with the semicollusive outcome. Competition implies that research at Stage 1 and production at Stage 2 are set non-cooperatively. This leads to the following amount of research and production for firm $i$:

$$q_i^N = \frac{(a - A)}{3b} \frac{4.5b\gamma}{4.5b\gamma - (2 - \beta)(1 + \beta)} \, , \tag{3.24}$$

$$x_i^N = \frac{(a - A)(2 - \beta)}{4.5b\gamma - (2 - \beta)(1 + \beta)} . \tag{3.25}$$

Semicollusion will in this case imply that firms collude at Stage 1 when setting R&D, and compete on Stage 2 when they set production. Given semicollusion, firm $i$'s research and production are as follows, respectively:

$$q_i^C = \frac{(a - A)}{3b} \frac{4.5b\gamma}{4.5b\gamma - (1 + \beta)^2} \, , \tag{3.26}$$

$$x_i^C = \frac{(a - A)(1 + \beta)}{4.5b\gamma - (1 + \beta)^2} \tag{3.27}$$

We can now compare the equilibrium values in those two regimes. It turns out that the spillover, modeled with the parameter $\beta$, is crucial for the outcome.[14] If spillover is low ($\beta < 1/2$), the amount of research is lower when they coordinate research than if they do not. The reason is obvious. Coordination makes it possible to avoid the competition on

---

[14] Henriques (1990) has shown that the equilibrium in the competitive regime is unstable if the spillover is sufficiently small ($\beta = 0.17$). See also d'Aspremont and Jacquemin (1990), where the role of $\beta$ is discussed.

R&D and thereby to save costs. However, for large spillover coordination leads to a larger amount of R&D. Spillover implies that own R&D leads to lower costs of production of its rival, an effect each firm does not take into account if they act non-cooperatively. This positive externality is internalized when they collude on R&D, and therefore they find it profitable to set a higher amount of R&D in order to lower both firms' costs of production. Suzumura (1992) has extended their model to an oligopolistic industry with more general demand and cost functions, and find that their main results are valid also in such a setting.[15]

The results concerning production and thereby prices follow straightforward from the equilibrium values of R&D. If they cut down on R&D, this leads to higher costs of production and thereby lower production and higher prices. This is true if the spillover is sufficiently low. For high spillover, the opposite is true. It implies that consumers are better off with semicollusion as long as the spillover is sufficiently large.

Interestingly, d'Aspremont and Jacquemin (1988) find that the firms will always gain from semicollusion. The semicollusive effect we have discussed earlier — tougher competition is triggered along another dimension — is not present in this setting. There is no reason to overinvest in R&D at Stage 1, to reap a larger benefit from a possible collusion on prices at a later stage. As noted in Fershtman and Gandal (1994), firms cannot be worse off under semicollusion than in the non-cooperative interaction as long as the collusion occurs at Stage 1.

### 3.3.1.2   Extensions of the Basic Model

Katz (1986) applies a more general model than in d'Aspremont and Jacquemin (1988).[16] In line with what we reported above, he finds that collusion on R&D is more likely to be beneficial for consumers if the spillover is large. Katz discusses in detail how various sharing rules

---

[15] For other extensions of the basic model, see among others de Bondt et al. (1992), Simpson and Vonortas (1994), Ziss (1994), de Bondt and Henriques (1995) as well as articles referred to in Section 3.3.1.2.

[16] See also Spence (1984), obtaining similar results by employing different formulations.

concerning costs and output affect the outcome. He finds, as we expect, that cost sharing leads to more R&D. However, he finds that output sharing may lead to less R&D. The reason is that each firm anticipates that it will help its rival to increase its production by undertaking own R&D, and this free rider effect dampens the incentives to invest in R&D. Finally, he finds that it is less likely with more R&D following collusion on R&D when competition is intense among firm. The reason is that intense rivalry leads to large investments in R&D, which implies that coordination of R&D leads to less R&D to avoid a costly battle for market shares.

It seems plausible that cooperation can make it possible with more spillovers, for example through the implementation of various sharing rules as in Katz (1986). Kamien et al. (1992) have made a more explicit analysis of the role of information sharing as such. They distinguish between four scenarios, where Scenario 1 and Scenario 2 are identical to the ones analyzed in d'Aspremont and Jacquemin (1988). In Scenario 3 and Scenario 4, which they denote research joint venture (RJV), they allow for information sharing concerning spillovers. It implies that the spillover is at a maximum, which in the previous model we discussed implies that $\beta = 1$. In Scenario 3, called RJV competition, they assume that they share information but that they set R&D non-cooperatively. In Scenario 4, which they call RJV cartelization, they share information and in addition set R&D that maximizes joint profit. It turns out that R&D is lowest in Scenario 3, when they share information and thereby have maximum spillovers but sets R&D non-cooperatively. Such a low investment in R&D is due to the free rider effect; each firm expect to free ride on other firms' R&D. On the other hand, Scenario 4 with information sharing and collusion on R&D typically leads to the highest amount of R&D. Then they realize that they can jointly gain from higher R&D, and therefore their joint decision on R&D leads to a large investment in R&D.

In contrast to those models described above, Choi (1992) considers both process and product innovations with stochastic outcomes. It is assumed that the spillover rate increases with cooperation on R&D. Since spillover leads to tougher competition in the product market, this implies that cooperation can be detrimental to profits. He finds that firms are better off colluding on R&D when spillover rates are high. Moreover, he finds that society would be better off if firms colluded even more on R&D than what is profitable for the firms.

Nocke (2007) applies a state-space approach where current investments in product improvements (product innovation) change future market conditions. In his model firms collude or compete on product R&D at Stage 1, and compete on quantities at Stage 2. Collusion on R&D leads to a low level of R&D, since they then by definition avoid an escalation in investments outlays. He finds that collusion on R&D is less likely the higher the spillover rate. With a high spillover rate each firm chooses a low non-collusive R&D level and ends up with low quality on its products in the non-collusive equilibrium. But underinvestment as a collusive outcome, with even lower level of R&D, can only be supported by a credible threat to expand R&D after any deviation. As shown in Nocke (2007), this threat is very limited with a large amount of spillover since the amount of R&D in the non-collusive outcome is close to the R&D level in the collusive outcome.

All the above-referred models assume that firms compete in the product market. However, collusion in R&D might lead to collusion in the product market. Martin (1995) has shown that this indeed can be the case.[17] He considers a trigger strategy where a breakdown of collusion in the product market leads to a breakdown of the collusion on R&D as well. R&D is undertaken because it is profitable as such for the firms. This implies that any deviation from a collusive outcome in the product market will trigger not only tough competition in the product market, but also competition on R&D. The punishment for deviating from a collusive price is thus larger when they collude on R&D than if they compete on R&D, which implies that there is a larger scope for collusion on prices when they also collude on R&D.

Martin (1995) assumes that cooperation on R&D is contractible and a commitment. However, it is often hard to write down and enforce R&D contracts. Cabral (2000) argues that R&D programs normally progress over a long period, it is difficult to contract on future actions,

---

[17] See also Lambertini et al. (2003). They extend Martin's approach, where process innovation was analyzed, by considering product innovation.

and each firm's contribution to R&D can be difficult to observe. He considers non-binding, self-enforcing agreements in a setting where there is scope for tacit collusion on both prices and R&D.[18] There is a probability that an investment in R&D leads to an improved technology. Success in R&D is a zero-one, once-for-all event, and R&D is assumed to be a public good (100 % spillovers). Although it is found that a monopoly price can be sustained, in some cases it is optimal for the firms to set a price below the monopoly price.[19] A low price will lead to low profits in the current period. This encourages the firms to invest heavily in R&D, and thereby increases the probability for a successful R&D investment. If R&D is successful, they move on to a price-setting subgame with no R&D. Moreover, he also shows that it can be possible with an equilibrium where firms choose low R&D to sustain collusive prices. The driving force behind this result is that after successful R&D it is assumed that it is hard to enforce a large punishment for deviation from a collusive price, either because capacity constraints are binding or products are more differentiated.

### 3.3.1.3 Public Policy Implications

While collusion on prices is illegal, cooperation on R&D has been treated much more favorable by competition authorities. The findings from the previous sections give some support for a more favorable public policy toward R&D cooperation than toward price fixing. Several of the theoretical studies find that with large spillovers cooperation on R&D can lead to more R&D and lower prices. For example, Kamien et al. (1992) find that R&D cooperation that leads to information sharing and thereby maximum spillovers are often welfare improving. Such a cooperation is expected to lead to high R&D investment, ensures that

---

[18] Cabral relates his study to the multimarket contact model in Bernheim and Whinston (1990). Although there are some notable differences, there is an analogy between competing in several markets and competing in different strategic variables. See also Cooper and Ross (2008), where it is argued that joint ventures in one market can facilitate collusion in another market.

[19] Note that Cabral (2000) finds that there is a multiplicity of equilibria. For example, one alternative could be to have a large probability to abandon any future R&D if no success having been reached. This threat of abandonment of R&D will sustain the efficient R&D investment.

all firms have access to discoveries on identical terms, and the low costs associated with high R&D leads to low prices in the product market. Semicollusion, where firms collude on R&D and compete on prices, is therefore expected to often be welfare improving.

However, there is one important caveat. Some studies show that cooperation on R&D might promote collusion on prices. Although it is shown that there are many possible outcomes when they can collude on both R&D and prices (see Cabral, 2000), this makes cooperation on R&D much more likely to be detrimental to welfare. If collusion on R&D leads to lower marginal costs and at the same time higher prices, we have the classical trade off first shown in Williamson (1968) concerning mergers. This is illustrated in Figure 3.4.

In Figure 3.4 we assume that cooperation on R&D leads to lower average costs, but at the same time higher prices. The latter leads to a dead weight loss that must be traded off against the gains for society from lower costs. If the dark shaded area is larger than the light shaded area, R&D cooperation (combined with collusion on prices) leads to lower total welfare. Note that in this model, where R&D is process innovation, consumers are worse off as long as prices go up. When R&D leads to product improvements, the net effect for consumers (and for society) is more complex.

Most competition authorities apply a consumer welfare standard. Given such an approach, they should ban process innovation as long

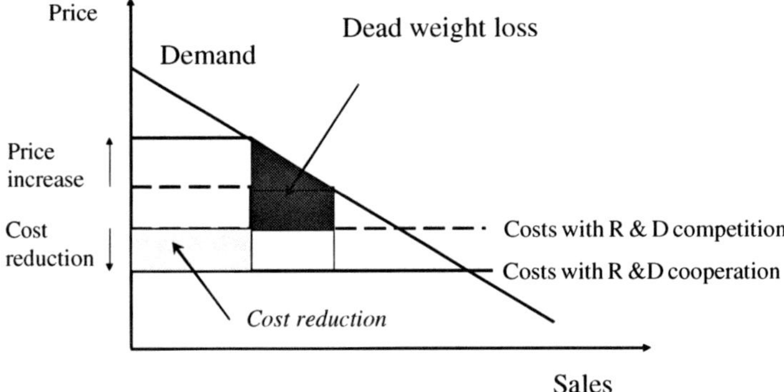


Fig. 3.4 The Williamson welfare tradeoff.

as prices go up. This indicates that cooperation on R&D should be allowed if it does not promote collusion on prices. The rules concerning R&D in for example Europe is favorable toward R&D cooperation, but it is not so obvious that the rules are able to disentangle between R&D that promote price collusion and R&D that does not promote price collusion. For example, the rules are concerned about market shares since firms with a combined market share below 25% are exempted from the Article 81 ban on cooperation between competing firms. A more natural approach would be to focus directly on aspects that favor price collusion as such. For example, in markets where firms have detailed knowledge about each others prices it might be good reason to expect a collusive price to be achieved. Another policy alternative, proposed by Hinloopen (1997), would be to subsidize R&D rather than allowing for collusion on R&D.

In many industries there are sector regulators, not only competition authorities, that can intervene. Sector regulators are often closer to a total welfare standard approach than a consumer welfare standard approach. If we apply a total welfare standard, the Williamson tradeoff is valid. It implies that a sector regulator following a total welfare standard will be more favorable toward collusion on R&D. Even if it leads to collusion on prices, it might be optimal to allow it. This illustrates that the choice of welfare standard can be crucial for the optimal public policy.

### 3.3.2 Collusion on Other Non-price Variables

Since competition law is restrictive toward collusion on prices and more favorable toward collusion along other dimensions, we would expect collusion on other choice variables than price. However, except for collusion on R&D there are few examples in the literature on collusion on non-price variables. As far as we know, there are only a few studies of collusion on advertising and a study of investment in infrastructure in telecom.[20]

---

[20] Foros et al. (2002) consider collusion on infrastructure in the telecom market and competition on prices. Their model, though, shares many of the features with some of the models we have discussed in the section on collusion on R&D and competition on prices.

Simbanegavi (2009) analyzes semicollusion where firms collude on advertising and compete on prices. He extends the model first introduced in Grossman and Shapiro (1984). Two firms are located equidistantly on a circular market. If consumers are not informed about any of the two firms' products, then they do not participate. Both firms advertise, and each consumer receives an ad from either none, both or one firm. If it receives ad from one firm, then it buys the product if it is individual rational to do so. If it receives ads from both firms, it chooses the one that leads to the highest surplus. In Grossman and Shapiro (1984), it is shown that more advertising leads to lower prices. The reason is that more advertising leads to more consumers being informed about both products. To capture those fully informed consumers, each firm has an incentive to lower its price.

Given that advertising triggers tougher competition on prices, it is no surprise that Simbanegavi (2009) finds that collusion on advertising leads to less advertising in equilibrium. It leads to a dampening of competition, and the firms earn higher profits both from higher prices and lower investments in advertising. However, the welfare effect of this kind of semicollusion is more complex to understand. There are cost savings due to lower outlays on advertising. On the other hand, consumers are worse off due to higher prices and worse off due to the fact that fewer customers are informed. Simbanegavi finds that the net effect on welfare from this kind of semicollusion is negative.

Aluf and Shy (2001) apply a model where advertising is not informative. In their model advertising leads to more differentiated products. In contrast to the results in the Grossman and Shapiro (1984) model, an increase in advertising leads to higher prices in the noncooperative equilibrium. They find that collusion on advertising leads to a higher level of advertising. The reason is that this will dampen price competition.

## 3.4  Semicollusion with Free Entry

In the discussion so far we have assumed a fixed number of firms. However, a change in the nature of competition, for example collusion rather than competition on prices, can lead to a change in the number of active firms. For example, higher profit is expected to attract entrants to the industry in question.

To our knowledge, there is only one study that investigates the consequences of semicollusion in a model with free entry. Symeonidis (2000a) builds on the models in Sutton (1991, 1998), and in contrast to Sutton's models he also considers how a change in the toughness of price competition affects the amount of advertising/R&D. He employs a vertical differentiation model, where a quality parameter can be interpreted as something that can be increased either by advertising or R&D. He assumes the following sequence of moves:

- *Stage 1: Firms decide to enter or not*
- *Stage 2: Firms set advertising/R&D*
- *Stage 3: Firms set prices*

He assumes that firms set advertising/R&D non-cooperatively at Stage 2, and investigates what happens if there is an exogenous change in the toughness of price competition at Stage 3.

It turns out that opposing forces are at work. We know from our earlier discussion, see for example Sections 3.1 and 3.2, that tougher price competition for a given number of firms leads to less investment in advertising or R&D. Since gross profits have fallen and at the same time fixed costs have fallen due to lower investment in the non-price variable, tougher price competition may lead to either more or less profits for a given number of firms. Hence, it is not clear whether semicollusion would lead to entry or exit of firms. Obviously, whether it is entry or exit is expected to be quite crucial for the change in total advertising/R&D in the industry following a change in the toughness of price competition.

Symeonidis (2000a) employs a specific model, and according to this model he finds by using simulations that tougher price competition leads to a lower amount of advertising/R&D in an industry with free entry. This result confirms the results reported previously, where we found that semicollusion where firms collude on prices typically leads to higher amounts of advertising and R&D (as well as capacities). However, Symeonidis admits that his results might be special to the functional forms he has employed.

It is of interest to go back to one of the first models we discussed, the capacity model in Fershtman and Gandal (1994). They found that semicollusion — with competition on capacities and collusion on prices — led to higher industry capacity and lower net profits. If we instead assume free entry, a shift to semicollusion is expected to lead to exit. Fewer firms will typically lead to less intense rivalry. Less intense rivalry will in this setting imply that they invest less in capacity. In theory one could therefore expect that semicollusion might lead to less, not more, investment in capacity.

While the capacity model in Fershtman and Gandal (1994) considered a duopoly, let us check the equilibrium values for $n$ number of firms. If competition, the equilibrium amount of capacity in the industry is the following:

$$k_i^N = q_i^N = \frac{1 - \gamma}{1 + n}. \tag{3.28}$$

If collusion on prices and competition on capacities, the amount of capacity in the industry is as follows given that there is the same number of firms:

$$k_i^C = q_i^C = \frac{n - 1}{4\gamma n^2}. \tag{3.29}$$

It can easily be shown that for a given number of firms, there will always be higher investment in capacities in a semicollusive outcome than in a competitive outcome.

However, we know from Fershtman and Gandal (1994) that in the semicollusive outcome with a fixed number of firms we have lower profits than in the competitive outcome. This will induce exit. Let us assume that $x$ firms exit following the establishment of semicollusion. With a slight abuse of notation, we assume that $x$ is a continuous variable. Comparing Equations (3.28) and (3.29), we have that the number of firms that must exit following the establishment of semicollusion for the level of industry capacity being unchanged is the following:

$$x = \frac{(1 - 4\gamma(1 - \gamma))n^2 - 1}{1 + n(1 - 4\gamma(1 - \gamma))}. \tag{3.30}$$

The number of firms that must exit for total industry capacity being unchanged depends on the number of firms initially and on the cost per unit of installing capacity. It is assumed that that $\gamma < 1/4$. If we set $\gamma = 0.23$ and $n = 4$, then total capacity goes down if semicollusion leads to exit of two firms. This suggests that in theory a model with free entry can lead to lower industry capacity after semicollusion is established. However, in this particular model it seems as if there must be a substantial exit for this to happen. This makes such an outcome quite unlikely, at least in our very specific model.

# 4

## Empirical Findings

In an empirical study of cartel profitability, Asch and Seneca (1976) found that cartels tended to be non-profitable. As shown in some of the theoretical models this can be consistent with the existence of semi-collusion, where cartels despite collusive prices waste their profits on non-profitable competition along other variables. Such a result raises the question why the firms in the first place collude on prices, since competition on all variables is more profitable. However, other studies indicate that collusion on prices is profitable, resolving this puzzle.[1] However, none of these studies test directly for semicollusion. There can be many other reasons why collusion is profitable (or not profitable).

In this section, we will primarily focus on those studies that test more directly for semicollusion than the one already mentioned. It turns out, though, that there are rather few such empirical studies

---

[1] See, for example, Griffin (1989). She analyzed 54 international cartels, and concluded that at least some of the cartels must have increased the profits of their members quite substantially. Levenstein (1997) found that the profits in the cartelized bromine industry were at least temporarily close to the joint profit-maximizing level. Griffin (2001) discusses the Lysine cartel, which was able to increase prices with more than 70% during its operation. She also refers to the graphite electrode cartel where US prices alone went up in excess of 60%.

and therefore we also refer to some empirical studies that test for semi-collusion more indirectly.

In the previous section we distinguished between (i) collusion on prices and competition on other choice variables and (ii) collusion on non-price variables and competition on prices. To make the link between the theoretical studies and empirical testing as simple as possible we follow the same structure in this section.

## 4.1 Collusion on Prices

### 4.1.1 Competition on Capacities

Most of the empirical studies of semicollusion have focused on capacity competition. There exist studies across several markets and time periods. Empirical studies explicitly focusing on semicollusion with capacity competition and price collusion include Ma (2008), Röller and Steen (2006), Salvanes et al. (2003), Steen and Sørgard (1999), and Dick (1992). In addition, there are studies that consider whether industries with collusion on prices typically carry more excess capacities than other industries, and in that respect test more indirectly for semicollusion.

Ma looks at a Taiwanese flour cartel in the period 1994–1998. Government imposed capacity sharing rules gave the firms incentives to collude on prices but at the same time compete on capacities to ensure a large market share. He estimates a simple conjectural variation model, and different market outcomes are simulated. It is found that the model with capacity competition and collusion on prices fits the data best.

Röller and Steen (2006) and Steen and Sørgard (1999) analyze a Norwegian cement cartel. Norway had since 1923 a monopolized domestic market with three large producers that organized sales through a joint sales office. The domestic market was shared according to each firm's share of total domestic capacity, and they used side payments to make sure that the sharing rule was met. Each firm was allowed to export cement. The export price they received was typically above short-run marginal costs, but did not cover costs of installing capacity. Each firm then might have incentives to expand domestic capacity in order to receive a large share of the domestic market. If investments

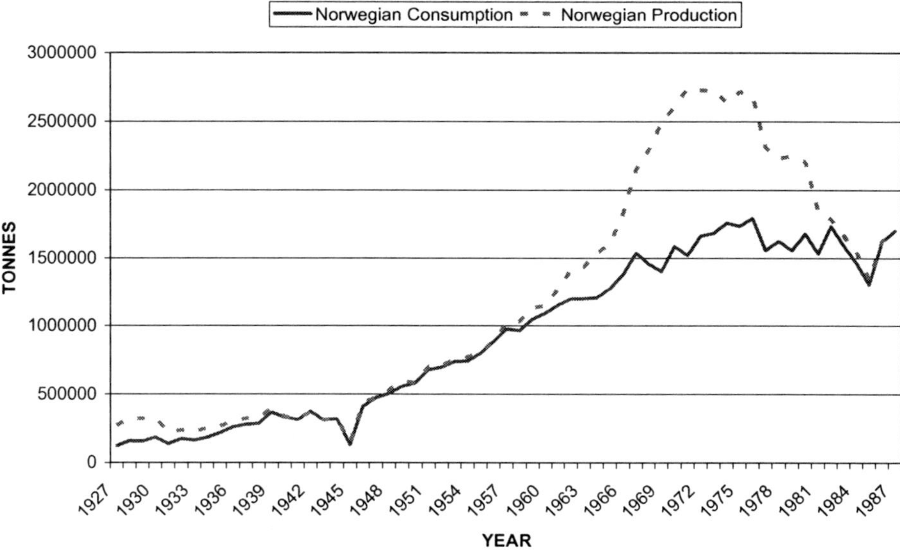


Fig. 4.1 Norwegian consumption and exports of cement 1927–1987.

in capacities exceed domestic demand we expect to observe exports. In Figure 4.1 we see that Norwegian production of cement exceeds Norwegian consumption in the 1920s and also from the late 1950s and until the early 1980s. In particular, we observe that production expanded a lot during the 1960s. One possible explanation for this expansion could be that the collusion on prices triggered large investments in capacity. As explained earlier, Lorange (1973) indicates that the lack of coordination on capacities led to large costs due to excess capacity and was an important reason for the merger to monopoly for those three firms in 1968.

In Steen and Sørgard (1999) they use data from 1927 to 1982 to test whether price collusion triggered capacity expansion. They extend Fershtman and Gandal (1994) to the case where firms have the alternative to export. Let $A$ denote size of the domestic market, and $E$ export volume. They show that if they collude also on capacity, then the prediction would be that $\partial E/\partial A < 0$. Larger domestic market would lead to a reallocation of sales from the export market to the domestic market. However, if the domestic market becomes sufficiently large and they collude on domestic prices but compete on capacity, then $\partial E/\partial A > 0$. Increased size of the domestic market would make it more profitable to expand capacities to capture a larger share of this market. Such an expansion would lead to larger exports. Steen and Sørgard test whether such a semicollusion effect is present. They find that it is not present prior to World War II, which is plausible given that the size of the domestic market was rather limited. However, they find that the semicollusive effect was present in the late cartel period 1956–1967.

Röller and Steen (2006) extend this study by constructing a structural model that they bring to data for the late cartel period. They confirm the results in Steen and Sørgard. In addition, they are able to undertake a welfare analysis of the cartel behavior. From the firm's first-order condition marginal costs can be identified simply from observing each firm's share of total capacity, the domestic price, and the export price. Estimating demand, they are now able to undertake a counter-factual analysis: what if monopoly instead of a price cartel, or what if Cournot competition instead of a price cartel? They find that the cartel actually performs worse than an uncoordinated Cournot oligopoly would have done by the end of the cartel's life span. They show that the merger to monopoly in 1968 even was welfare enhancing compared to the semicollusive cartel. At this point the export loss due to excess capacity that had to be utilized for non-profitable exports was so high that even though domestic consumers lost in terms of higher prices, total welfare was actually improved. This is illustrated in Figure 4.2.

In Salvanes et al. (2003) the competition in the Norwegian airline market after deregulation in 1994 is scrutinized. The two Norwegian airline companies apparently colluded on price through a neat setup with interlining meetings, signaling in media and very transparent pricing systems. However, they fought to gain market shares by investing in excess capacity (and as we will see later also flight location). Using a data set on route level for the period 1985–1995 including city pairs with different competitive structure (monopoly versus duopoly) they are able to model the market and test predictions on semicollusion. They find support for a semicollusive effect, implying that the firms expanded capacity in excess of what they would have done if the competed on both prices and capacities.

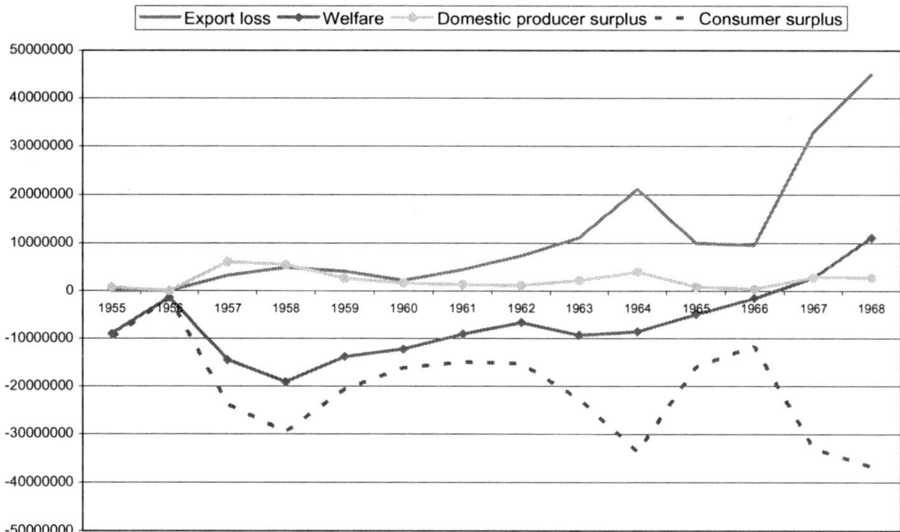


Fig. 4.2 Impact of moving from a cartel to a monopoly (Source: Figure 7 Röller and Steen, 2006).

Dick (1992) analyzes Japanese export cartels across a lot of different industries for the period 1950–1985. All of these had minimum price arrangements. His results are consistent with semicollusion in the sense that the industries that had the most successful cartel performance also had typically additional horizontal agreements on 'maximum quantity' and therefore prevented semicollusion to take place. Of 12 cartelized industries, 4 were found to perform well, of those, 3 had both price and capacity restrictions imposed.

There are other empirical studies of the relationship between excess capacity and prices. Rosenbaum (1989) and Conlin and Kadiyala (2007) analyze the US aluminum industry and the Texas lodging industry, respectively. The starting point in both studies is the theory of collusion, where excess capacity can be used to support a collusive price. However, their empirical testing does not check for causality. This means that any relationship between prices and excess capacity could have the reverse causality, where high prices trigger investments in capacity. Rosenbaum finds that high prices are correlated with excess capacity, while Conlin and Kadiyali find that high prices are correlated with symmetric distribution of excess capacity. In both studies the conclusion is that this is consistent with a theory of collusion where excess capacity supports high prices. However, their findings are also consistent with a model where collusion on prices trigger competition on capacities.

Another study of the relationship between capacity and prices is Symeonidis (2003). He uses a four-digit industry data from UK from the 1950s and the 1960s. It is found that capacity intensive industries are more likely to collude. One interpretation of this study is that UK industries colluded only on prices, and therefore they competed on other choice variables such as, for example, capacities.

The main studies related to semicollusion on capacity are tabulated in Table 4.1.

### 4.1.2   Competition on R&D

As we will see later (see Section 4.2.1), there are some empirical studies of collusion on R&D and competition on prices. However, to our knowledge there are only one empirical study that tests directly for whether there is collusion on prices and competition on R&D.

A recent study by Günster et al. (2009) provides a direct test of R&D competition and product market collusion. They analyze the performance of cartels in the period 1983–2004 that were fined by European Commission for colluding on prices. They estimate reduced form models, and they confirm that firms that have been involved in cartels have been able to raise profits in cartel years. They also look at R&D expenditures, and find that there are significant increases in these during cartelization years. This indicates that collusion on prices seems to be paralleled by increases in R&D expenditures. If so, there is a semicollusive effect where collusion on prices triggers tougher competition on R&D to capture market shares. Interestingly, this outcome is a puzzle for the authors. They conclude that '*R&D expenditures show the most surprising results indicating an increase in R&D expenditures during cartel years.*'

Although there are few direct tests of collusion on prices and competition on R&D, the literature on the inverse U-shaped curve concerning

Table 4.1. Competition on capacity.

| Author(s) | Market | Collusion variable | Competition variable | Dataset period | Modeling approach | Results | Sharing rule |
|---|---|---|---|---|---|---|---|
| Dick (1992) | Japanese export cartels in several industries | Price | Capacity | 1950–1985 | Estimate reduced form price and quantity equations | Cartels performing best had also quantity/ capacity restrictions imposed in addition to minimum price | Explicitly agreed capacity sharing rules |
| Steen and Sørgard (1999) | Norwegian cement | Price | Capacity | 1927–1982 | Estimate export supply relations and test model predictions | Semicollusion was triggered by the growth in the domestic market after World War II | Explicitly agreed capacity sharing rule with side payments and joint sales office |
| Salvanes et al. (2003) | Norwegian airlines | Price | Capacity | 1985–1995 | Estimate capacity utilization regressions across city pairs with different competition status and test model predictions | Semicollusion is found on the biggest citypair duopoly routes | Assumed that more capacity increases market share |
| Röller and Steen (2006) | Norwegian cement | Price | Capacity | 1956–1982 | Estimate structural model and perform welfare analysis | Semicollusion is found to be even more detrimental to welfare than a non-coordinated Cournot oligopoly just prior to merger | Explicitly agreed capacity sharing rule with side payments and joint sales office |
| Ma (2008) | Taiwanese Flour | Price | Capacity | 1994–1999 | Conjectural variation model simulated market outcomes | The simulated semicollusive regime fits the data best | Government imposed capacity sharing rule |

innovation might be of interest. Both theoretical and empirical studies find that innovation is higher with medium concentration than what is the case with either monopoly (very high concentration) of low concentration.[2] The explanation for this relationship is analogous to our explanation when firms collude on prices and compete on R&D. Higher concentration leads to a dampening of competition and thereby higher price–cost margin. This triggers more intense rivalry for market shares through investment in R&D. In contrast, we are concerned about how R&D will be affected when firms shift from competing to colluding on prices for a given concentration in an industry. Despite the question we raise is not identical, the results in the empirical literature on the inverse U-shaped curve are consistent with our predictions from theory of semicollusion. Fewer firms lead to a larger potential for collusion on prices, which implies that a shift toward a more concentrated industry can lead to a shift toward collusion on prices.

### 4.1.3  Competition on Location

There are a number of studies trying to explore the effects of product differentiation and concentration, either in the form of concentration indexes or in the form of number of firms. Examples of such studies include Netz and Taylor (2002) and Götz and Gugler (2006), who both analyze gasoline station differentiation. Netz and Taylor find evidence of differentiation increasing in the number of firms, whereas Götz and Gugler find that concentration reduces product variety.[3] There are, however, no studies explicitly addressing semicollusion when it comes to location competition. The studies coming closest to this are Stavins (1995), Borenstein and Netz (1999) and Salvanes et al. (2005).

Stavins is modeling entry and exit in the US personal computer (PC) market. Using hedonic price regressions and a product differentiation measure they estimate entry and exit models over a large panel

---

[2] See, for example, Aghion and Griffith (2005).

[3] There are also some studies addressing location choice and price competition in gasoline retailing that focus on density, prices, and firm concentration. Not surprisingly the main result is that prices are reduced in the number of local stations, but it is hard to find significant effects from firm concentration. See, e.g., Clemenz and Gugler (2006) and Meerbeeck (2003).

over the period 1976–1988. The PC market has changed over this period from being oligopolistic to becoming more of a market with monopolistic competition. One might ask whether the change in competition led to a change in product characteristics competition as well. In particular one might ask whether it should be more entry deterrence (i.e., filling up niches before the competitors have the time to do so) in a situation with more competition. However, when they separate the panel into early and late they find no evidence of any difference in product differentiation.

In the same fashion Borenstein and Netz test for the scheduling of flight departures. As explained in Section 3.2.3, if collusion on prices we can expect that firms locate close to each other. In a market with more than two firms the theoretical prediction could be that we observe pairwise location, in our case that pairwise flights are located close to each other in time (called clustering). They estimate flight differentiation equations across two different regulation (competition) regimes in the US airline industry. In the old era (1975) both prices and partly also frequencies were regulated, while in the new era (1986) the industry was fully deregulated. Thus, one might anticipate a potential semicollusion effect taking place in flight location for the regulated era. In line with the model we presented in Section 3.2.3.2, one prediction would be that collusion on prices would lead to pairwise location of flights and thereby what is denoted clustering of flights in the old era. Their results are unclear. They do not find substantially more clustering in the regulated era, where prices were fixed, when also considering the frequency regulation effects at the time.[4]

Salvanes et al. (2005) are also testing for the time scheduling of flight departures. They analyze the Norwegian airline market before and after deregulation in 1994. The two airline companies apparently colluded on price on flexible tickets also after deregulation (see above). However, one prediction could be that they fought to gain market shares by

---

[4] Berry and Waldfogel (2001) analyze how mergers and a dampening of competition in local radio broadcasting in the USA led to increased variety in programming content. They find clear evidence that the programming content variety increased after the 1996 Telecommunication Act due to a consolidation in this industry leading to substantially more concentration in local radio station ownership.

locating the flights close to each other. Salvanes et al. apply a data set before and after deregulation in April 1994, comparing 1991–1993 with 1995–1997. Their data cover several city pair routes with different competitive structure across routes and time (monopoly versus duopoly). By formulating a flight clustering index and regress this on controls as departures, passengers, and competitive route status, they find clear evidence of increased clustering of flights on duopoly routes. This suggests that semicollusion took place on scheduling of flight departures, where collusive prices encouraged the airlines to locate close to its rival.[5]

Interestingly, they find clearer results when looking at the business segment where the collusion on prices on flexible tickets is most important. Finally, it is shown that typically it is the entering firm on a route that locates close to the incumbent after entry, being the main source of the clustering and semicollusion effect. On monopoly routes that stayed monopoly throughout the data period, flights were found to be significantly more spread out.

The main studies related to semicollusion on location are tabulated in Table 4.2.

### 4.1.4  Competition on Advertising

Symeonidis (2000a, 2000b) is modeling how short-run price competition influences advertising or R&D expenditures. He applies a reduced form model on UK industry data from the 1950s and 1960s to test whether a tougher price competition led to less advertising or less R&D. If the answer is yes, this is consistent with semicollusion where tougher price competition triggers softer competition on those two other choice variables.

In the 1950s UK competition authorities imposed a more restrictive practice by no longer allowing firms to engage in price fixing. Symeonidis (2000b) uses the exogenous shift toward a more restrictive practice to test how collusion on prices affects advertising expenditure.

---

[5] Note that using a somewhat larger data set on capacity utilization they also found price collusion also triggered tough competition on capacities (see Salvanes et al., 2003, reported in Section 4.1.1).

Table 4.2. Competition on location.

| Author(s) | Market | Collusion variable | Competition variable | Data set period | Modeling approach | Results | Sharing rule |
|---|---|---|---|---|---|---|---|
| Stavins (1995) | US personal computer market | Price | Product characteristics PCs | 1976–1988 | Using hedonic price regressions and measures of product differentiation they regress entry/exit across a panel of brands/PCs | Estimate separate models for early (oligopoly) and late (monopolistic competition), find no significant differences across these periods | |
| Borenstein and Netz (1999) | US airline industry | Price | Location of flights | 1975 and 1986 | Estimate differentiation (clustering of flights) regressions across routes | Unclear on the semicollusion effect: The price regulated regime (1975) seems not to be suggesting more flight crowding than the unregulated regime (1986) when also considering the frequency regulation effects at the time | Assumed that customers are distributed according to capacity and time schedules |
| Salvanes et al. (2005) | Norwegian airlines industry | Price | Location of flights | 1991–1997 | Estimate waiting time (clustering) regressions across city pairs with different competition status | The companies cluster their flights on duopoly routes | Assumed that customers are distributed according to capacity and time schedules |

He finds that the shift toward a more restrictive practice leads to a reduction in advertising expenditure, which is consistent with semi-collusion. However, his results depend on which data set he applies. Symeonidis (2000a) is not testing his model, but he presents a case study that is in line with the predictions from his model. The UK refrigerator industry had a non-price competition agreement that ended in the 1960s. In 1958, when they still colluded, the advertising expenditure was as high as 3.5–4% of sales revenue. Ten years later when they also competed on prices this figure was reduced to 1.1% of sales revenue.

Wang et al. (2007) construct a theoretical model where the firms can compete/collude either on advertising or price (see Section 3.2.4). They use weekly data from the US butter and margarine industry to estimate a structural (AIDS) model, where they allow for different outcomes (e.g., competition/collusion in price/advertising). Using Vuong tests they find the model that fits the data best. Interestingly, the model which allows for collusion in advertising and competition in price fits the data best. They argue that this is a superior outcome, since collusion on advertising is less obvious and so far has not been aimed by the competition authorities as much as price collusion. Another interesting feature in their work is that they allow advertising to differ according to spillover effects: How much does firm $i$'s advertising also raise firm $j$'s sales. They argue that the higher the spillovers, the higher the incentives to collude.

Nicklisch (2008) tests the effect of the distinction between low and high investment spillovers in an experimental setting. He finds that the degree of advertising spillovers (high/low) affects to which degree investment collusion influences negatively the degree of price collusion. This study suggests that the degree of spillovers is important to the degree of semicollusion.

Slade (1995) analyzes the market for 'saltine crackers'. She uses a state space approach that makes it possible to accommodate all future effects rather than only the static setting in most other models. It is found that the firms compete vigorously on advertising and accommodate each other on prices, resulting in more advertising and higher prices than what would have been observed in a static game. However, this outcome is not necessarily due to semicollusion. She also states that despite the market outcome looks like overt collusion on prices in a static context, allowing dynamics the outcome is a result of non-cooperative actions.

The main studies related to semicollusion on advertising are tabulated in Table 4.3.

### 4.1.5   Competition on Other Variables

There exist some studies that test for various forms of competition that suggest the existence of semicollusion, but where the results are not denoted as semicollusion. One example is Ramrattan's (2001) study of the US car market where he tests the effects of dealership differentiation. He finds some empirical evidence in favor of semicollusion. In particular, he finds that the dealerships compete in number of dealership, advertising, and R&D outlays but not in price. He has, however, a reduced form approach estimating single equations for each of the big car brands with some conflicting results across brands.

Another interesting market is ocean liner shipping, where cartels have been institutionalized over a long time through so-called 'conferences'. Members typically charge identical prices, but engage in non-price competition along other dimensions such as frequency of departures, duration of voyages, and ship size (Fox, 1994). These 'conference cartels' are exempted from antitrust laws. Some conferences are more complicated also involving agreement on capacity, etc., but these are a lot more infrequent (Deltas et al., 1999). Interestingly, Deltas et al. find that the more tightly a conference is organized the better are their performance. This suggests conferences that are competing on factors other than price leads to lower profits. The authors apply a cross-sectional data on America's trade immediately before the outbreak of World War I, using simple single regression techniques where they analyze how the tightness of the conference is influenced by market characteristics.

During the 1970s the American Federal Trade Commission (FTC) ran a 'shared monopoly' case against the ready-to-eat cereal producers in the USA. Here the argument was that they were colluding on price but competed on brand proliferation. A large number of brands acted

Table 4.3.  Competition on advertising or price.

| Author(s) | Market | Collusion variable | Competition variable | Data set period | Modeling approach | Results | Sharing rule |
|---|---|---|---|---|---|---|---|
| Roberts and Samuelson (1988) | US cigarette market | Advertising | Price | 1971–1982 | Dynamic demand and cost functions, conjectural variation approach | Find evidence of joint profit maximization on advertising | Assumed that more advertising increases market share and/or increases total market demand |
| Symeonidis (2000b) | Cross-section UK four-digit industries | Price or quantity | Advertising | 1954–1973 | Reduced form estimation of advertising intensity equations | Collusion results in significantly higher advertising intensity | Assumed that more advertising increases market share |
| Symeonidis (2000a) | Case study UK refrigerator industry | Price or quantity | Advertising | 1958–1968 | Case study | Advertising exp. fell from 3.5–4% of sales revenue in 1958 to 1.1% in 1968 | Assumed that more advertising increases market share |
| Gasmi et al. (1992) | Coca-Cola and Pepsi-Cola | Advertising or price | Advertising or price | 1968–1986 | Estimate full information maximum likelihood versions of cost and demand functions. Use nonnested statistical tests to distinguish between the various competitive regimes | Their tests support the regime where there is collusion on advertising but not on price | Assumed that more advertising increases market share |

(*Continued*)

Table 4.3. (*Continued*)

| Author(s) | Market | Collusion variable | Competition variable | Data set period | Modeling approach | Results | Sharing rule |
| --- | --- | --- | --- | --- | --- | --- | --- |
| Wang et al. (2007) | US butter and margarine market | Advertising | Price | 1998–2002 | Structural system using AIDS | The model fitting the data best is one where firms compete in price but accommodate in advertising | Assumed that more advertising increases market share depending on the degree of spillovers |
| Nicklisch (2008) | Experimental study | Price or Quantity | Advertising | | Simple regressions using treatment groups | Weak evidence of semicollusion when advertising spillovers are high | Assumed that more advertising increases market share depending on the degree of spillovers |

as a barrier to entry. Most notably this was described by Schmalensee (1978) and later also in Scherer (1980). This resembles a seemingly semicollusive outcome with collusion on prices and competition along other dimensions.

Nevo (2001) analyzes this industry. He uses new empirical discrete choice models where he extends the BLP (Berry–Levinsohn–Pakes) approach, and use this approach to estimate demand and inferring price–cost margins based on 65 different US cities over the period 1988–1992. He concludes that if any significant price collusion existed, the observed margins would have been much higher. Assuming Nash–Bertrand as a benchmark of noncollusive pricing, he concludes that prices are not a result of collusive behavior. He finds that the high margins are primarily due to the producer's ability to maintain a portfolio of differentiated brands and influence the perceived quality of these brands by means of advertising. However, his models are not dealing with the potential anti-competitive effects of the brand proliferation strategy of these firms, thus leaving the potential anti-competitive effects of this strategy an open question.

The main studies related to semicollusion on other variables and R&D are tabulated in Table 4.4.

## 4.2 Competition on Prices

### 4.2.1 Collusion on R&D

There are rather few studies on collusion on R&D and product market competition. There are some studies that estimate what are the determinants of research joint ventures (RJV), where product market competition is controlled for using concentration numbers like the Herfindahl index (Röller et al., 2007; Hernán et al., 2003). Röller et al. find a positive relationship between HHI and R&D growth, whereas Hernán et al. find that HHI positively influences the likelihood of entering an RJV. This suggests that in concentrated markets RJVs are more likely. If there is a positive correlation between potential product market collusion and concentration, this suggests that there might be a link between collusion on R&D and collusion on price. Two more recent

Table 4.4. Competition on other variables.

| Author(s) | Market | Collusion variable | Competition variable | Data set period | Modeling approach | Results | Sharing rule |
|---|---|---|---|---|---|---|---|
| Deltas et al. (1999) | American ocean liner shipping | Price | Frequency, speed, tonnage | 1912–1914 | Reduced form single regressions | The most tightly organized cartels ('conferences') found to perform better than the simpler price cartels | Assumed that higher frequency/ speed/ tonnage increases market share |
| Nevo (2001) | US ready-to-eat cereal market | Price | Brand pro-liferation/ advertis-ing | 1988–1992 | Extend structural BLP modeling estimating demand inferring price cost margins | High margins are primarily due to the producer's ability to maintain a portfolio of differentiated brands and influence the perceived quality of these brands by means of advertising, not collusion on prices | Brand proliferation increases market shares and prevent entry |
| Ramrattan (2001) | US car dealership | Price | Number of dealer-ships, advertis-ing, R&D outlays | 1970–1996 | Reduced form single regressions | Find some evidence across car brands for competition on number of dealerships, advertising, and R&D outlays | Assumed that higher number of dealerships, more advertising, or higher R&D outlays increase market share |

studies of RJV formation and potential product market competition focus exactly on this.

Seldeslachts et al. (2008) use a somewhat similar approach as Röller et al., and they find that large RJVs in concentrated industries are more stable and hence more prone to facilitate product market collusion. Goeree and Helland (2008) have a different approach in the sense that they use the shift in competition policy in the USA (leniency program) to see whether the relationship between RJV participation and concentration changes after leniency was introduced. The idea is that if product market collusion is not a motivation to form an RJV the propensity to enter into an RJV should not be affected by this change. They find a lower RJV-participation after the policy change (collusion being now less attractive with leniency introduced), and Goeree and Helland argue that this implies that RJVs can support collusion on prices.

The critical assumption underlying all these studies is the assumed positive link between concentration and collusion. Even though most will argue that this is the case, there is no one-to-one correspondence established here and therefore one should be cautious when interpreting these results in terms of product market collusion. Furthermore, the change in RJV participation in the USA after 1993 might also be due to other factors than only the introduction of leniency. Finally, the studies are difficult to reinterpret into a semicollusion setting. As we saw in Section 3.3.1, the model predictions depend on, e.g., the degree of spillovers, something we do not know anything about from these empirical studies.

### 4.2.2   Collusion on Other Non-price Variables

In many countries collusion on prices is illegal, whereas collusion on advertising is not. We saw previously that Wang et al. (2007) found advertising collusion to be more in line with their data on the margarine and butter industry, and Nicklisch (2008) focused on the spillovers that are possible when the collusion variable is advertising rather than other variables as capacity and location.

Collusion on advertising is even promoted in some countries like for milk products in the USA. The potential illegality of advertising collusion is therefore evaluated on a case-by-case basis using a *rule of reason* approach (Simbanegavi, 2009). See for instance Lande and Marvel (2000) for a discussion of the case between FTC and the California Dental Association that had imposed restrictions on advertising and was finally allowed to continue doing so. A corresponding case is the decision by the FTC where they ruled against an advertising restriction agreement between Warner and Polygram regarding the advertisements of the first two 'Three Tenors' albums in the 1990s (see Goldberg, 2005).[6] The two record companies had each been responsible for one (very successful) album, and now when launching a joint third concert they wanted to minimize potential advertising 'noise' when planning the marketing of the third album. This advertising restriction was, however, ruled to be illegal by the FTC.

When turning to econometric studies, one can interpret Roberts and Samuelson (1988) analysis of the US cigarette industry as a test of semicollusion. They develop a dynamic model of *nonprice* competition where they allow collusion on advertising, where the latter can affect both firm market shares and the total size of the market. They cannot reject the hypothesis of joint profit maximizing on advertising as the best model for the data period 1971–1982. They argue that their results suggest that excessive advertising due to a prisoners' dilemma game has been avoided in this industry.

Gasmi et al. (1992) provide more empirical evidence of collusion on advertising and competition on prices. They look at different possible market configurations in the Coca-Cola and Pepsi-Cola market; Stackelberg leadership, Nash behavior and collusion on one or both price and advertising. They use data for the period 1968–1986 to estimate a full information maximum likelihood version of cost and demand functions and use non-nested statistical tests to distinguish between the various regimes to determine which fits the data best. They find support for collusion on advertising but not on price.

---

[6] The 'Three Tenors' were the famous opera singers Luciano Pavarotti et al., that through three concerts during the 1990s ended up producing three famous concert albums. The first two were very successful, in particular the first that ended up being the best-selling classical record ever (Goldberg, 2005).

# 5

## Some Concluding Remarks

Semicollusion is an important phenomenon in numerous industries, illustrated by a large amount of anecdotal evidence that we have referred to in this survey. In many of these anecdotes it is suggested that collusion on one choice variable leads to tougher competition on other choice variables. Our survey shows that we can find support for such a claim in both theoretical and empirical studies. However, when we go into the detail in our survey we see that the picture is more mixed than what we can read from the anecdotes.

In particular, it is important to distinguish between colluding on prices and colluding on non-price variables. If collusion on prices, most theoretical models assume that this takes place on the last stage of the game. Given collusion on prices in the last stage of the game, firms can set non-price variables prior to that in order to get a larger share of the market. For example, both theoretical and empirical studies show that firms in many industries have invested heavily in capacity prior to colluding on prices in order to get a large share of the collusive profit. This can even lead to lower profits for the firms than in a competitive outcome. In that respect Stigler (1968) was right when he asked if *'any monopoly profit achieved by suppressing price competition be eliminated by non-price competition?'*

On the other hand, there are examples where competition on non-price variables followed by collusion on prices is profitable for the firms. For example, this is true when they compete on R&D and the spillovers are sufficiently large.

More importantly, collusion on non-price variables followed by competition on prices has a distinctly different effect than collusion on prices and competition on other choice variables. According to the theoretical literature it is no longer true that collusion on one choice variable triggers tough competition on other choice variables. On the contrary, it has been argued — in particular concerning R&D — that collusion on one non-price variable may lead to collusion on prices. If so, allowing for partly collusion might lead to full collusion. This illustrates that semicollusion can have qualitatively different effects depending on which choice variable they collude on.

We find that the welfare effects of semicollusion can in theory be ambiguous. Apparently, if collusion on prices triggers tougher competition on other non-choice variables this might imply that consumers and society can be better off compared to a competitive outcome. However, this need not be true. Tougher competition can lead to waste — as we see when they install capacity that becomes idle — or to a distortion in the positioning of products we see in some location models. This suggests that the general skeptical view we have on price collusion could in many cases be strengthened, although the ambiguity implies that in some cases the triggering of tougher competition can be beneficial for both consumers and society. It is interesting to note that only one empirical study actually tests the welfare implications of semicollusion. The theoretical ambiguity therefore suggests a scope for more work on this question.

On the other hand, we question the way collusion on R&D has been exempted from competition law in many countries. From theory it seems as a natural exemption, given that this does not encourage firms to collude on prices as well. This suggests that whether those firms should be allowed to collude on R&D should depend on whether there is a potential for collusion prices in that particular industry. Instead of focusing on joint market shares, as they do in the present regime in for example Europe, they should focus on, for example, firms which are symmetric in size and where the industry is transparent.

The survey has revealed that there are some issues that are under-researched, in the theoretical and even more so in the empirical literature. In the theoretical literature we see that (i) collusion on prices and competition on capacities and (ii) collusion on R&D and competition/collusion on prices are investigated in detail. This indicates that there is scope for developing more basic models of some possible semicollusive outcomes, in particular investigating the consequences of collusion on prices and competition on advertising. Moreover, many of the semicollusion models are two-stage games wherein the second game is a static price game where monopoly price is set. One important avenue for further research would be to test what would happen if the last stage of the game is modeled as an infinite repeated price game.

The empirical literature on semicollusion is more limited than the theoretical literature. Although the number is rather limited, there are more empirical studies on collusion on prices and competition on capacities than most other situations with semicollusion. This shows that collusion on prices and competition on capacities is well documented both theoretically and empirically. In addition, there are in relative terms many empirical studies of collusion on prices and competition on advertising. In contrast, there are rather few theoretical studies on this issue. The fact that we observe most empirical studies focusing on advertising, and capacity competition might be due to the more obvious link between market share competition and these variables. In addition, data availability might play a role since for instance R&D competition and location is potentially harder to empirically model and obtain data on.

From our survey, it is thus obvious that there is scope for future research on this topic. For example, given that collusion on R&D is such an important issue in the theoretical literature it is despite potential data limitations a puzzle that there are almost no empirical studies of this market outcome. Furthermore, numerous anecdotes suggest that collusion on prices and competition on advertising is quite common, but there are very few theoretical studies of this nature of competition.

# References


Aghion, P. and R. Griffith (2005), *Competition and Growth. Reconciling Theory and Evidence*. The MIT Press.

Aluf, Y. and O. Shy (2001), 'Comparison-advertising and competition'. Mimeo, University of Haifa, Israel.

Asch, P. and J. J. Seneca (1976), 'Is collusion profitable?'. *Review of Economics and Statistics* **58**(1), 1–12.

Benoit, J.-P. and V. Krishna (1987), 'Dynamic duopoly, prices and quantities'. *Review of Economic Studies* **54**(1), 23–35.

Benoit, J.-P. and V. Krishna (1991), 'Entry deterrence and dynamic competition: The role of capacity reconsidered'. *International Journal of Industrial Organization* **9**, 477–495.

Bensaid, B. and A. DePalma (1993), 'Spatial multiproduct oligopoly'. Working Paper.

Bernheim, B. D. and M. D. Whinston (1990), 'Multimarket contact and collusive behaviour'. *RAND Journal of Economics* **21**, 1–16.

Berry, S. T. and J. Waldfogel (2001), 'Do mergers increase product variety? Evidence from radio broadcasting'. *The Quarterly Journal of Economics* pp. 1009–1025.

Blisard, N. (1999), 'Advertising and what we eat: The case of dairy products'. *Advertising: Dairy*, USDA/ERS pp. 181–188.

Bloch, K. (1932), 'On German cartels'. *The Journal of Business* **5**, 213–222.

Borenstein, S. and J. Netz (1999), 'Why do all flights leave at 8 am?: Competition and departure-time differentiation in airline markets'. *International Journal of Industrial Organization* **17**, 611–640.

Bos, I. and J. E. Harrington, Jr. (2010), 'Endogenous cartel formation with heterogeneous firms'. *RAND Journal of Economics*, forthcoming.

Brander, W. and R. Harris (1984), 'Anticipated collusion and excess capacity'. Mimeo, University of British Colombia.

Brod, A. and R. Shivakumar (1999), 'Advantageous semicollusion'. *Journal of Industrial Economics* **47**, 221–230.

Cabral, L. (2000), 'R&D cooperation and product market competition'. *International Journal of Industrial Organization* **18**, 1033–1047.

Chamberlin, E. (1929), 'Duopoly: Value where sellers are few'. *Quarterly Journal of Economics* **43**, 63–100.

Chang, M.-H. (1991), 'The effects of product differentiation on collusive pricing'. *International Journal of Industrial Organization* **9**, 453–469.

Chang, M.-H. (1992), 'Intertemporal product choice and its effect on collusive firm behaviour'. *International Economic Review* **33**, 773–793.

Choi, J. P. (1992), 'Cooperative R&D with product market competition'. *International Journal of Industrial Organization* **11**, 553–571.

Clemenz, G. and K. Gugler (2006), 'Locational choice and price competition: Some empirical results for the Austrian retail gasoline market'. *Empirical Economics* **31**, 291–312.

Conlin, M. and V. Kadiyala (2007), 'Capacity and collusion: An empirical analysis of the Texas lodging industry'. Mimeo, Michigan State University.

Cooper, R. W. and T. W. Ross (2008), 'Sustaining cooperation with joint ventures'. *Journal of Law, Economics & Organization* **25**(1), 31–54.

Dasgupta, P. and E. Maskin (1986), 'The existence of equilibrium in discontinuous economic games, II: Applications'. *Review of Economic Studies* **53**, 27–41.

d'Aspremont, C., J.-J. Gabszewicz, and J. Thisse (1979), 'On Hotelling's "Stability in Competition"'. *Econometrica* **47**, 1145–1150.

d'Aspremont, C. and A. Jacquemin (1988), 'Cooperative and noncooperative R&D in duopoly with spillovers'. *American Economic Review* **78**, 1133–1137.

d'Aspremont, C. and A. Jacquemin (1990), 'Cooperative and non-cooperative R&D in duopoly with spillovers: Erratum'. *American Economic Review* **80**, 641–642.

Davidson, C. (1983), 'The competitive effect of segmented markets'. *California Law Review* **71**, 445–463.

Davidson, C. and R. Deneckere (1984), 'Excess capacity and collusion'. Mimeo, Michigan State University.

Davidson, C. and R. Deneckere (1990), 'Excess capacity and collusion'. *International Economic Review* **31**(3), 521–541.

de Bondt, R. and I. Henriques (1995), 'Strategic investment with asymmetric spillovers'. *Canadian Journal of Economics* **28**(3), 656–674.

de Bondt, R., P. Slaets, and B. Cassiman (1992), 'The degree of spillovers and the number of rivals for maximum effective R&D'. *International Journal of Industrial Organization* **10**, 35–54.

Deltas, G., K. Serfes, and R. Sicotte (1999), 'American shipping cartels in the pre-world War I era'. *Research in Economic History* **19**, 1–38.

Dick, A. R. (1992), 'The competitive consequences of Japan's export cartel associations'. *Journal of the Japanese and International Economics* **6**, 275–298.

Eaton, B. C. and R. C. Lipsey (1975), 'The Principle of Minimum Differentiation Reconsidered: Some New Developments in the Theory of Spatial Competition'. *Review of Economic Studies* **42**, 27–49.

Eckard, E. W. (1991), 'Competition and the cigarette TV advertising ban'. *Economic Inquiry* **29**, 119–133.

Ericson, R. and A. Pakes (1995), 'Markov-Perfect industry dynamics: A framework for empirical work'. *Review of Economic Studies* **62**, 53–82.

Fershtman, C. and N. Gandal (1994), 'Disadvantageous Semicollusion'. *International Journal of Industrial Organization* **12**, 141–154.

Fershtman, C. and E. Muller (1986), 'Capital investment and price agreement in semicollusive markets'. *Rand Journal of Economics* **17**, 214–226.

Fershtman, C. and A. Pakes (2000), 'A dynamic oligopoly with collusion and price wars'. *RAND Journal of Economics* **31**, 207–236.

Foros, Ø., B. Hansen, and J. Y. Sand (2002), 'Demand-side spillovers and semicollusion in the mobile communications market'. *Journal of Industry, Competition and Trade* **2**(3), 259–278.

Fox, N. R. (1994), 'An oligopoly model of ocean liner shipping'. *Review of Industrial Organization* **9**, 343–355.

Friedman, J. M. and J.-F. Thisse (1993), 'Partial collusion fosters minimum product differentiation'. *RAND Journal of Economics* **24**, 631–645.

Gabszewicz, J. and J.-F. Thisse (1986), 'Spatial Competition and the Location of Firms'. In: J. Gabszewicz, J.-F. Thisse, M. Fujiata, and U. Schweizer (eds.): *Location Theory*. London: Harwood Academic Press.

Gasmi, F., J. J. Laffont, and Q. Vuong (1992), 'Econometric analysis of collusive behavior in a soft drink market'. *Journal of Economics and Management Strategy* **1**, 277–311.

Goeree, M. S. and E. Helland (2008), 'Do research ventures serve a collusive function?'. Mimeo.

Goldberg, V. P. (2005), 'Featuring the three tenors La Triviata'. *Review of Law and Economics* **1**, 55–64.

Götz, G. and K. Gugler (2006), 'Market concentration and product variety under spatial competition: Evidence from retail gasoline'. *Journal of Industry, Competition, and Trade* **6**, 225–234.

Griffin, J. M. (1989), 'Previous cartel experience: Any lessons for OPEC?'. In: L. R. Klein and J. Marquez (eds.): *Economics in theory and practice: An eclectic approach*. Dordrecht, Kluwer, pp. 179–206.

Griffin, J. M. (2001), 'An inside view at a cartel at work: Common characteristics of international cartels'. In: A. Sundberg (ed.), chapter 3: *Fighting cartels — why and how?* Stockholm, Swedish Competition Authority.

Grossman, G. M. and C. Shapiro (1984), 'Informative advertising with differentiated products'. *Review of Economic Studies* **51**, 63–81.

Günster, A., M. Carree, and M. Van Dijk (2009), 'The performance of European cartels 1983-2004: An investigation of the effects of cartel formation on profitability, productivity and innovativeness'. EARIE 2009.

Henriques, I. (1990), 'Cooperative and non-cooperative R&D in duopoly with spillovers: Comment'. *American Economic Review* **80**, 638–640.

Hernán, R., P. L. Marin, and G. Siotis (2003), 'An empirical evaluation of the determinants of research joint venture formation'. *The Journal of Industrial Economics* **51**, 75–89.

Hinloopen, J. (1997), 'Subsidizing cooperative and non-cooperative R&D in duopoly with spillover'. *Journal of Economics* **66**(2), 151–175.

Hotelling, H. (1929), 'Stability in Competition'. *Economic Journal* **34**, 41–57.

Jèhiel, P. (1992), 'Product differentiation and price collusion'. *International Journal of Industrial Organization* **10**, 633–641.

Kamien, M., E. Muller, and I. Zang (1992), 'Research joint ventures and R&D cartels'. *American Economic Review* **82**, 1293–1306.

Kaplow, L. and C. Shapiro (2007), 'Antitrust'. In: A. M. Polinsky and S. Shavell (eds.): *Handbook in Law and Economics*, vol. 2. Oxford, UK, North-Holland.

Katz, M. L. (1986), 'An analysis of cooperative research and development'. *RAND Journal of Economics* **17**(4), 527–543.

Kreps, D. and J. Scheinkman (1983), 'Quantity precommitment and bertrand competition yield cournot outcome'. *Bell Journal of Economics* **14**, 326–337.

Lambertini, L., S. Poddar, and D. Sasaki (2003), 'RJVs in product innovation and cartel stability'. *Review of Economic Design* **7**, 465–477.

Lande, R. H. and H. P. Marvel (2000), 'The three types of collusion: Fixing prices, rivals and rules'. *Wisconsin Law Review* pp. 941–99.

Levenstein, M. C. (1997), 'Price wars and the stability of collusion: A study of the pre-World War I bromine industry'. *Journal of Industrial Economics* **45**, 117–137.

Levenstein, M. C. and V. Y. Suslow (2008), *Cartels, The New Palgrave Dictionary of Economics*. Macmillan, 2nd edition.

Lorange, P. (1973), 'Anatomy of a complex merger: A case study and analysis'. *Journal of Business Finance* **5**, 32–38.

Ma, T.-C. (2008), 'Disadvantageous collusion and government regulation'. *International Journal of Industrial Organization* **26**, 168–185.

Martin, S. (1995), 'R&D joint ventures and tacit product market collusion'. *European Journal of Political Economy* **11**, 733–741.

Martin, S. (2001), *Industrial Organization — A European perspective*. Oxford University Press.

Martinez-Giralt, X. and D. J. Neven (1988), 'Can price competition dominate market segmentation?'. *Journal of Industrial Economics* **36**, 431–442.

Matsui, A. (1989), 'Consumer benefited cartels under strategic capital investment competition'. *International Journal of Industrial Organization* **7**, 451–470.

Meerbeeck, W. V. (2003), 'Competition and local market conditions on the Belgian Retail Gasoline Market'. *De Economist* **151**(4), 369–388.

Mukherjee, A. (2002), 'Advantageous and disadvantageous semicollusion'. KERP 2002/10, Keele University.

Netz, J. S. and B. A. Taylor (2002), 'Maximum or minimum differentiation? Location patterns of retail outlets'. *The Review of Economics and Statistics* **84**(1), 162–175.

Nevo, A. (2001), 'Measuring market power in the ready-to-eat cereal industry'. *Econometrica* **69**, 307–342.

Nicklisch, A. (2008), 'Semicollusive advertising and pricing in experimental duopolies'. Preprints of the Max Planck Institute for Research on Collective Goods, Bonn, 2008/25, http://ssrn.com/abstract=1161076.

Nocke, V. (2007), 'Collusion and (under)-investment in quality'. *RAND Journal of Economics* **38**, 227–249.

Osborne, M. J. and C. Pitchik (1987), 'Cartels, profits and excess capacity'. *International Economic Review* **28**(2), 313–328.

Phlips, L. (1962), *De l'intègration des marches*. Louvain and Paris, Nauwelaerts.

Phlips, L. (1995), *Competition Policy: A Game-theoretic Perspective*. Cambridge University Press.

Ramrattan, L. B. (2001), 'Dealership competition in the US automobile industry'. *American Economist* **45**(1), 33–45.

Rawls, J. (1971), *A Theory of Justice*. Cambridge, Massachusetts: Harvard University Press.

Roberts, M. J. and L. Samuelson (1988), 'An empirical analysis of dynamic, nonprice competition in an oligopolistic industry'. *RAND Journal of Economics* **19**(2), 200–220.

Röller, L.-H., R. Siebert, and M. M. Tombak (2007), 'Why firms form (or do not form) RJVs'. *The Economic Journal* **117**, 1122–1144.

Röller, L.-H. and F. Steen (2006), 'On the Workings of a Cartel: Evidence from the Norwegian Cement Industry'. *American Economic Review* **96**, 321–338.

Rosenbaum, D. I. (1989), 'An empirical test of the effect of excess capacity in price setting, capacity-constrained supergames'. *International Journal of Industrial Organization* **7**, 231–241.

Ross, T. W. (1992), 'Cartel stability and product differentiation'. *International Journal of Industrial Organization* **10**, 1–13.

Rotschild, R. (1997), 'Product differentiation and cartel stability: Chamberlin versus hotelling'. *The Annals of Regional Science* **31**, 259–271.

Salvanes, K. G., F. Steen, and L. Sørgard (1997), 'Hotelling in the air? Flight departures in Norway'. SNF, Working Paper 48/1997.

Salvanes, K. G., F. Steen, and L. Sørgard (2003), 'Collude, compete, or both? Deregulation in the Norwegian airline industry'. *Journal of Transport Economics and Policy* **37**, 383–416.

Salvanes, K. G., F. Steen, and L. Sørgard (2005), 'Hotelling in the air? Flight departures in Norway'. *Regional Science and Urban Economics* **35**, 193–213.

Scherer, F. M. (1970), *Industrial Market Structure and Economic Performance*. Rand McNally & Company, Chicago.

Scherer, F. M. (1980), *Industrial Market Structure and Economic Performance*. Houghton Mifflin Company.

Scherer, F. M. and D. Ross (1990), *Industrial Market Structure and Economic Performance*. Houghton Mifflin Company.

Schmalensee, R. (1978), 'Entry deterrence in the ready-to-eat breakfast cereal industry'. *The RAND Journal of Economics* **9**, 305–327.

Schmalensee, R. (1987), 'Competitive advantage and collusive optima'. *International Journal of Industrial Organization* **5**, 351–367.

Schmalensee, R. (1994), 'Sunk costs and market structure: A review article'. *Journal of Industrial Economics* **40**, 125–134.

Seldeslachts, J., T. Duso, and E. Pennings (2008), 'On the stability of research joint ventures: Implications for collusion'. Mimeo.

Simbanegavi, W. (2009), 'Informative advertising: Competition or cooperation?'. *Journal of Industrial Economics* **57**, 147–166.

Simpson, R. D. and N. S. Vonortas (1994), 'Cournot equilibrium with imperfectly appropriable R&D'. *Journal of Industrial Economics* **42**(1), 79–92.

Slade, M. (1995), 'Product rivalry with multiple strategic weapons: An analysis of price and advertising competition'. *Journal of Economics & Management Strategy* **4**(3), 445–476.

Spence, M. (1984), 'Cost reduction, competition, and industry performance'. *Econometrica* **52**, 101–121.

Stavins, J. (1995), 'Model entry and exit in a differentiated-product industry: The personal computer market'. *The Review of Economics and Statistics* **4**, 571–584.

Steen, F. and L. Sørgard (1999), 'Semicollusion in the Norwegian cement industry'. *European Economic Review* **43**, 1775–1796.

Stigler, G. (1968), 'Price and non-price competition'. *Journal of Political Economy* **76**, 149–154.

Sutton, J. (1991), *Sunk Cost and Market Structure*. Cambridge, The MIT Press.

Sutton, J. (1998), *Technology and Market Structure: Theory and History*. Cambridge: The MIT Press.

Suzumura, K. (1992), 'Cooperative and non-cooperative R&D in an oligopoly with spillovers'. *American Economic Review* **82**, 1307–1320.

Symeonidis, G. (2000a), 'Price and non-price competition with endogenous market structure'. *Journal of Economics & Management Strategy* **9**, 53–83.

Symeonidis, G. (2000b), 'Price competition, Non-price competition and market structure: Theory and evidence from the UK'. *Economica* **67**, 437–456.

Symeonidis, G. (2003), 'In which industries is collusion more likely? Evidence from the UK'. *The Journal of Industrial Economics* **51**, 45–74.

Sørgard, L. (1997), 'Judo economics reconsidered: Capacity competition, entry and collusion'. *International Journal of Industrial Organization* **15**(3), 349–368.

Tennant, R. B. (1950), *The American Cigarette Industry: A Study in Economic Analysis and Public Policy*. Yale University Press: New Haven.

Tirole, J. (1988), *The Theory of Industrial Organization*. Cambridge: The MIT Press.

Tyagi, R. K. (1999), 'On the relationship between product substitutability and tacit collusion'. *Managerial and Decision Economics* **20**, 293–298.

Vasconcelos, H. (2005), 'Tacit collusion, cost asymmetries, and mergers'. *RAND Journal of Economics* **36**, 39–62.

Wang, S.-S., T. P. Dahr, and K. W. Stiegert (2007), *Semicollusive Market Outcomes: Theory and Evidence*. Mimeo, University of Wisconsin-Madison.

Whish, R. (2003), *Competition Law*. LexisNexis, London, 5th edition.

Williamson, O. (1968), 'Economies as an antitrust defense: The welfare tradeoffs'. *American Economic Review* **58**(1), 18–36.

Ziss, S. (1994), 'Strategic R&D spillovers, collusion and welfare'. *Journal of Industrial Economics* **42**(4), 375–393.

Lightning Source UK Ltd.
Milton Keynes UK
04 June 2010

155120UK00001B/36/P